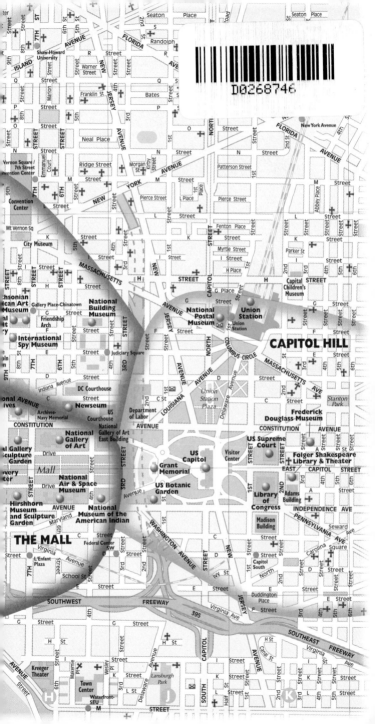

CITYPACK TOP 25
Washington

MARY CASE AND BRUCE WALKER
ADDITIONAL WRITING BY MATTHEW CORDELL

AA Publishing
If you have any comments or suggestions for this guide you can contact the editor at
travelguides@TheAA.com

How to Use This Book

KEY TO SYMBOLS

✠ Map reference to the accompanying fold-out map	❓ Other practical information
✉ Address	▷ Further information
☎ Telephone number	ℹ Tourist information
🕐 Opening/closing times	✋ Admission charges: Expensive (over $9), Moderate ($4–$9), and Inexpensive ($3 or less)
🍴 Restaurant or café	
🚉 Nearest rail station	⭐ Major Sight ★ Minor Sight
Ⓜ Nearest subway (Metro) station	👣 Walks 🚌 Excursions
🚌 Nearest bus route	🛍 Shops
🚢 Nearest riverboat or ferry stop	🎭 Entertainment and Nightlife
♿ Facilities for visitors with disabilities	🍴 Restaurants

This guide is divided into four sections
• **Essential Washington:** An introduction to the city and tips on making the most of your stay.
• **Washington by Area:** We've broken the city into six areas, and recommended the best sights, shops, entertainment venues, nightlife and restaurants in each one. Suggested walks help you to explore on foot.
• **Where to Stay:** The best hotels, whether you're looking for luxury, budget or something in between.
• **Need to Know:** The info you need to make your trip run smoothly, including getting about by public transportation, weather tips, emergency phone numbers and useful websites.

Navigation In the Washington by Area chapter, we've given each area its own color, which is also used on the locator maps throughout the book and the map on the inside front cover.

Maps The fold-out map accompanying this book is a comprehensive street plan of Washington. The grid on this fold-out map is the same as the grid on the locator maps within the book. We've given grid references within the book for each sight and listing.

Contents

Introducing Washington

Equal parts Southern gentility, Northern sophistication and power politics, America's capital is a microcosm of the United States, the melting pot's melting pot. Washington DC is both quintessentially American and unique as an American city.

Washington is a city of contradictions because it was a compromise from the start. The site was chosen, close to George Washington's home at Mount Vernon, after a deal was brokered for the South to pay the North's revolutionary war debts in exchange for having a southern capital. Virginia and Maryland donated land for the District, and architect Pierre Charles L'Enfant (1754–1825) designed a city with a focal triangle formed by the Capitol, the president's house and a statue where the Washington Monument now sits.

L'Enfant also included plans for the Mall and wide diagonal boulevards crossing the grid of streets. L'Enfant's magnificent vision can be appreciated now, but for a long time this city was little more than a sparsely populated swamp with empty avenues. Cattle grazed on the Mall and America's famous early leaders worked in and inhabited dank, dilapidated buildings.

This city, rich in contradictions, is as a result, rich in things to see. Capitol Hill and the Mall, replete with free museums, galleries and monuments, exhibit the magnificence of America's wealth and artistry. The revitalized U Street and Columbia Heights reveal its cultural dynamism. Embassies have brought foreign delegations and friends, imbuing this relatively small city with pockets of cuisine and culture unavailable elsewhere in the US. And a quickly burgeoning arts scene, in part fueled by the droves of young professionals that move to the capital clamoring for powerful positions, is suprisingly sophisticated. Washington is America's amusement park.

Facts + Figures

- The 508ft (154m) escalator at the Wheaton Metro station is the longest in the Western Hemisphere.
- The Pentagon, at 6.6 million sq ft (613,000sq m), is the world's third largest building by floor area and has 17.5 miles (28.2km) of corridors.

TAXATION, REPRESENTATION?

Washington DC license plates read "Taxation without Representation," a familiar refrain from the Revolutionary War. In this case the term alludes to the fact that the District lacks a voting representative in Congress. To add insult to injury, the Constitution also specifically gives Congress control over Washington's entire budget.

DC ON FIRE

On August 25, 1814, as part of the ongoing War of 1812, British soldiers entered Washington and began torching the town. They destroyed many buildings, including the Capitol and the White House, but not before dining on a feast First Lady Dolley Madison hubristically prepared before being forced to leave. Both buildings still retain scars from the incident.

SECOND SUBWAY

Members of Congress in a rush to vote need not break a sweat. In 1909, underground subway cars were installed to traverse the little more than 500ft (150m) between the Russell Senate Office Building and the Capitol. As subsequent office buildings were added, so were more train lines. These cars, most still open-top, continue to operate today.

A Short Stay in Washington

DAY 1

Morning Start your day in **Union Station** (▷ 62) and grab some coffee in the food court or a more formal breakast at the café in the main hall. Follow the flood of "Hill staffers" (▷ 123) as they head to work just before 9am. Most of them will stop at the Senate Office Buildings. You should, too, if you have arranged a tour with a Member of Congress office in advance. Otherwise head to the Capitol Guide Service Kiosk between the **Capitol** (▷ 60) and the **Botanic Garden** (▷ 58). Take a tour of the Capitol.

Lunch Head west out of the Capitol and onto the Mall. Either enjoy a meal of Native American delicacies at the **National Museum of the American Indian** (▷ 44) or one themed on the newest exhibit in the café of the East Building of the **National Gallery of Art** (▷ 43).

Afternoon Stay on after lunch and take in an exhibit at either museum, neither of which will disappoint.

Mid-afternoon Walk west along the Mall past the Smithsonian museums to the **Washington Monument** (▷ 46). Head up to the top (it's best to reserve tickets in advance) to catch a spectacular view of the city. On coming back down to earth walk due north to **The White House** (▷ 25).

Dinner Walk up to Farragut North Metro station and take the train downtown to the Gallery Place–Chinatown Metro station. Head west on G Street for Mediterranean tapas at the light, airy and lively **Zaytinya** (▷ 32).

Evening After dinner, grab drinks at **Rosa Mexicano** (▷ 32) or **Indebleu** (▷ 30) before taking in a show at the **Shakespeare Theatre** (▷ 30) or **Woolly Mammoth** (▷ 30), depending on whether you like the Bard or avant garde.

DAY 2

Morning Start off the day at the **National Zoological Park** (▷ 84). Be sure to say hello to the panda, the orangutans on the "O line" and the Komodo dragon, the first to be born outside of Indonesia.

Mid-morning Walk south on Connecticut Avenue and hop on the Metro to **Dupont Circle** (▷ 87). Or, if you made it a short stay at the zoo, walk across the Calvert Street Bridge and take an immediate right down 18th Street through **Adams-Morgan** (▷ 92).

Lunch If it's warm, try one of the outdoor cafés near the Metro's north entrance or on 17th Street, or take a picnic to the Circle. There are also many good indoor options on Connecticut Avenue north and south of the Circle and P Street west of the Circle.

Afternoon Take the Metro to the Smithsonian station. Walk toward the **Washington Monument** (▷ 46) to 15th Street SW and take a left, heading toward the Tidal Basin, where you will find the **FDR** and **Jefferson memorials** (▷ 37).

Mid-afternoon Walk from the FDR Memorial north to the Reflecting Pool and the **Lincoln Memorial** (▷ 39), where Martin Luther King Jr. delivered his "I Have a Dream" speech in 1963.

Dinner Enjoy the carefully crafted food at the restaurants in the **Mandarin Oriental hotel** (▷ 112): **CityZen** (▷ 52) if you want to go all out or the Empress Lounge if you're looking for something more casual.

Evening Catch a taxi to the **John F. Kennedy Center** (▷ 74), where, depending on the night, you can choose between ballet, opera, the symphony and world-class theater, among other things.

Top 25

▶▶▶

ESSENTIAL WASHINGTON TOP 25

Arlington National Cemetery ▷ 98–99
National heroes, like JFK, are buried here.

Cedar Hill ▷ 100 This is the former home of the anti-slavery abolitionist Frederick Douglass.

FDR and Jefferson Memorials ▷ 37 Two beautiful memorials to two revered statesmen.

The White House ▷ 25
This icon is both the president's home and his office.

Washington Monument ▷ 46–47 Windows in the top of this iconic obelisk offer panoramic city views.

Vietnam Veterans Memorial ▷ 48 A powerful memorial to the soldiers killed and missing in action in Vietnam.

US Supreme Court Building ▷ 63 An austere building where monumental cases are decided.

US Holocaust Memorial Museum ▷ 45 An unforgetable memorial to the millions exterminated by the Nazis in World War II.

US Capitol ▷ 60–61
Important debates of the day rage under this famous dome, which is also a showcase of Americana.

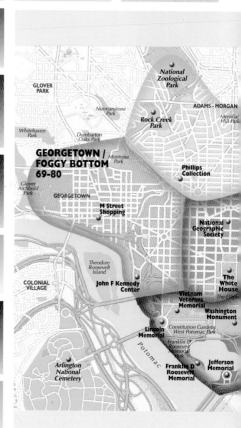

US Botanic Garden ▷ 58–59 This elegant conservatory houses tropical and subtropical plants from around the world.

Union Station ▷ 62 A bustling Beaux Arts transportation terminal and shopping center, with restaurants and a cinema.

Shrine of the Immaculate Conception ▷ 101 This gigantic Catholic church houses a 3-million-tile mosaic image of Jesus.

8

These pages are a quick guide to the Top 25, which are described in more detail later. Here they are listed alphabetically, and the tinted background shows which area they are in.

Freer and Arthur M. Sackler Galleries ▷ **38**
Some of the finest Asian art in the West.

Georgetown Shopping ▷ **73** DC's rich and powerful live and shop amid these tree-lined streets.

John F. Kennedy Center ▷ **74** Washington's premier performing arts center; world-class performances. ▼▼▼

Library of Congress ▷ **57**
Jefferson's former collection is now a temple to the written word.

Lincoln Memorial ▷ **39**
A somber monument to a complicated president.

National Air and Space Museum ▷ **40–41**
Soaring displays trace the progress of man reaching for the stars.

National Archives ▷ **42**
America's scrapbook offers a first-hand peek at history.

National Gallery of Art ▷ **43** A treasure house of European and American art.

National Museum of the American Indian ▷ **44**
Educational exhibits on America's first inhabitants.

National Geographic Society ▷ **24** Stunning exhibits on our planet are displayed vividly.

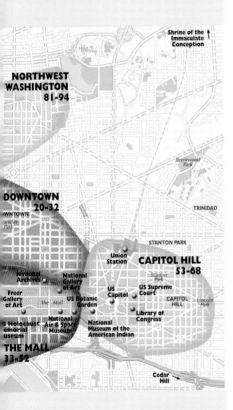

NORTHWEST WASHINGTON 81–94

Shrine of the Immaculate Conception

Brentwood Park

DOWNTOWN 20–32
WNTOWN
anklin Park

TRINIDAD

STANTON PARK

Union Station

CAPITOL HILL 53–68

Stanton Park

National Archives

National Gallery of Art

Freer Gallery of Art

US Botanic Garden

US Capitol

US Supreme Court

CAPITOL HILL

Lincoln Park

The Mall

National Air & Space Museum

Holocaust emorial useum

National Museum of the American Indian

Library of Congress

THE MALL 33–52

Cedar Hill

Rock Creek Park ▷ **86**
This wooded gorge in the heart of Washington DC is popular with hikers, bikers and joggers.

Phillips Collection ▷ **85**
Renowned collection of modern art in Phillips's Georgian revival mansion.

National Zoological Park ▷ **84** The public's park is home to more than 2,400 animal species.

◀◀◀

Shopping

For those who see Washington as a wonky, button-down city, the abundance of DC shopping options, from high-end showrooms to funky boutiques, might come as a surprise. Those with style and money to prove it will find shops like Chanel, Tiffany and Co. and Louis Vuitton in Friendship Heights and Chevy Chase. Vintage hunters can rummage for deals along the Adams-Morgan strip, on U Street or in Eastern Market on Capitol Hill. Mainstreamers will find solace in their favorite stores Downtown, in Georgetown and Pentagon City. Antiques and art hounds should head to Georgetown or Dupont Circle. Hip hard-to-find styles for body and home can be found on Book Hill in Georgetown and on U Street.

Bookworms

This city has not shortchanged its inordinate number of policy experts, think tanks and foundations with a lack of reading material. The major chains—Barnes & Noble, Borders, Books-a-Million and the local Olssons—are all well-represented, but bookworms will also find some unbeatable independents, such as Kramerbooks and Politics & Prose, that often include comfortable cafés and reading areas among their eclectic collections. Specialty shops—including those that cater to gays and lesbians, history buffs and specialists, among countless others—are also abundant.

Broaden the Mind

In fact, DC is generally the place to go if you're looking for something to broaden your mind.

PATTERNS FROM AFRICA

You may be intrigued by the vibrant hues and patterns of the kente cloth clothing worn by chic African-Americans in DC. Hand-woven in Ghana, it's available in bolts to sew with or made up into outfits from several good sources. Start your search at the National Museum of African Art (☎ 202/786–2147).

Georgetown (top and middle) and the window display of the French Market (bottom)

Aside from being a visual cornucopia for students of any age, the city's many museums and galleries contain gift shops and bookstores that extend experience and the learning process. The National Museum of the Native American stocks an expansive collection of Native American crafts, games and books. The National Building Museum carries a huge library of books on DC and the building arts. Many art museums around town, including the National Gallery of Art and the Hirshhorn, sell items ranging from exhibit catalogs to artisanal jewelry to high-quality prints. The Air and Space Museum carries glow-in-the-dark stars and freeze-dried astronaut food. And the Museum of Natural History stocks beautiful housewares alongside science kits.

Memorabilia

Likewise, nearly every government building and monument—including the White House, the Capitol, the Library of Congress and the Lincoln Memorial—sell American memorabilia.

Regional Delights

Washington is a good place to buy food and household items culled from the surrounding regions: Virginia peanuts; ham from North Carolina, Virginia and Kentucky; Pennsylvania quilts and Appalachian handicrafts such as handmade brooms and corn-husk dolls.

Georgetown (top); Chanel store (top middle); fresh crabs (middle); stylish shoes (bottom)

POLITICAL EPHEMERA

Election year or not, DC is a ready source of campaign ephemera—buttons, bumper stickers, matchbooks with party logos and the like. At bookstores, museum gift shops and street vendors, reproductions and original memorabilia abound. Looking for pewter flatware and candlesticks used by 18th-century administrations? A tacky T-shirt commenting on the latest Washington scandal? Who can resist the salt and pepper shakers shaped like the Washington Monument or campaign buttons designed for FDR? For this kind of Americana, there's no place like DC.

Shopping by Theme

Whether you're looking for a department store, a quirky boutique, or something in between, you'll find it all in Washington. On this page shops are listed by theme. For a more detailed write-up, see the individual listings in Washington by Area.

ART AND ANTIQUES

Georgetown Antiques Center (▷ 77)
Good Wood (▷ 90)
Hemphill Fine Arts (▷ 90)
Jean Pierre Antiques (▷ 77)
National Gallery of Art (▷ 52)
The Old Print Gallery (▷ 77)
Torpedo Factory Art Center (▷ 104)

BOOKS

Bridge Street Books (▷ 77)
Capitol Hill Books (▷ 66)
Kramerbooks (▷ 90)
Lambda Rising (▷ 90)
Reiter's Books (▷ 29)
Second Story Books (▷ 91)

FOOD AND WINE

A Litteri (▷ 66)
Calvert Woodley Liquors (▷ 90)
Cowgirl Creamery (▷ 29)
Dean and Deluca (▷ 80)
Eastern Market (▷ 64, 66)
Marvelous Market (▷ 94)

FOR KIDS

Dawn Price Baby (▷ 66)
Fairy Godmother (▷ 66)
Museum of Natural

History (▷ 52)
National Air and Space Museum (▷ 52)
National Museum of the American Indian (▷ 52)

HOME FURNISHINGS

Alvear Studio (▷ 66)
A Mano (▷ 77)
Anthropologie (▷ 77)
Bed Bath & Beyond (▷ 29)
Design Within Reach (▷ 77)
IKEA (▷ 104)
Miss Pixie's (▷ 91)
Muléh (▷ 91)
Tabletop (▷ 91)

MALLS

Fashion Center (▷ 104)
Friendship Heights (▷ 104)
Gallery Place (▷ 29)
Potomac Mills Mall (▷ 104)
Tyson's Corner (▷ 104)
Union Street (▷ 66)

MENSWEAR

American Apparel (▷ 29)
Carbon (▷ 90)
J. Press (▷ 29)
Puma (▷ 77)
Thomas Pink (▷ 91)

MISCELLANEOUS

Backstage, Inc (▷ 66)
Beadazzled (▷ 90)
Blue Mercury (▷ 90)
Coffee and the Works (▷ 90)
Fahrney's Pens (▷ 29)
Grooming Lounge (▷ 29)
House of Musical Traditions (▷ 104)
Kiehl's (▷ 77)
Music Box Center (▷ 29)
Paper Source (▷ 77)
Takoma Underground (▷ 104)

WOMENSWEAR

American Apparel (▷ 29)
Ann Taylor Loft (▷ 29)
Anthropologie (▷ 77)
Betsy Fisher (▷ 90)
Coup de Foudre (▷ 29)
Filene's Basement (▷ 29)
Forecast (▷ 66)
Hu's Shoes (▷ 77)
Intermix (▷ 77)
Meeps Fashionette (▷ 91)
Nana (▷ 91)
Pink November (▷ 91)
Proper Topper (▷ 91)
Rizik Brothers (▷ 91)
Secondi (▷ 91)
Thomas Pink (▷ 91)
Urban Chic (▷ 77)
The Village Gallery (▷ 66)

Washington by Night

The mix of illuminated white-marble and hard-working youngsters looking for relief after work makes Washington a vibrant place at night. Hot spots around town are busy early and stay open late even some weeknights, especially in the warmer months when people seek outdoor and rooftop seating.

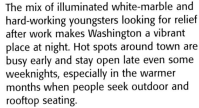

Going Out
Young professionals tend to head to areas like U Street and Chinatown, the hot spots of the moment; Dupont Circle; Adams-Morgan, which can get overcrowded with the 20-something crowd; Capitol Hill—quick access after work; and the area around the Clarendon Metro stop in Arlington, where many Hill staffers live. More mature diners and revelers tend to stick to the suburbs, especially Bethesda and Alexandria. But Washington DC feels like a town where everyone is in college—senators are even "junior" and "senior." People of all ages and interests socialize together.

Monuments in the Moonlight
If you don't feel like partying, a tour by car or on foot can be equally stimulating. The monuments and memorials, glorious in the sunlight, are entrancing in the moonlight. The Capitol looms on its hill over the Mall. The Lincoln Memorial stands guard at one end of Memorial Bridge, as does the Jefferson Memorial at the Tidal Basin. And the stark white Washington Monument is visible from most points in town.

Some of the many ways to spend an evening in Washington (above)

NAVAL OBSERVATORY
On selected Mondays, the US Naval Observatory, where astronomers made measurements in preparation for the Apollo moon missions, offers a peek at the stars through its 12-inch refracting telescope. Tours start at 8.30pm and include talks on the history of the Observatory and with a member of its Time Service Department, which maintains an atomic clock. Reservations should be made 4–6 weeks in advance; www.usno.navy.mil/USNO/tours-events).

Eating Out

Washington has long been home to dark-paneled, meat-and-potatoes places popular among older lawmakers and the lobbyists eager to ply them. But, in recent years, droves of young people have inspired restaurateurs to open good, inexpensive options as well as given them the freedom to push the culinary envelope in an effort to sate increasingly adventurous tastes.

Top Chefs

Benefiting from lush swaths of nearby farmland, the seafood-rich Chesapeake Bay and undeniable talent, chefs like Eric Zeibold (at CityZen), José Andrés (at Zaytinya, Jaleo, Oyamel and Café Atlantico), Cathal Armstrong (at Restaurant Eve) and Michel Richard (at Citronelle) are truly taking cuisine to new levels. Their restaurants and others no longer have to be qualified as simply "good for DC," they're objectively a treat. And this is just the beginning. As once funky areas of Washington become more gentrified, top chefs are following. Although you can generally expect a short wait during the week, don't make the mistake of going out without reservations on Friday or Saturday nights anywhere in town.

International Cuisine

Washington DC's diverse population hailing from all countries and states has spawned a restaurant scene that spans a wide array of options at a wide range of prices. Home to the second largest population of Ethiopians outside of Ethiopia, DC dishes out more than its share of this east African cuisine, especially in Georgetown, Adams-Morgan and Shaw. Likewise, a sizeable El Salvadorian crowd has set up restaurants and *pupuserias* in Mount Pleasant and Columbia Heights. In addition, West African, Thai, Chinese, Greek, Lebanese and Indian cuisines, among countless others, put up a good fight for their fair share of restaurant space. And don't forget that this is a southern city; soul food abounds.

Mouthwatering fruit salad (top); fusion food and fine cuisine (middle); alfresco dining (bottom)

Restaurants by Cuisine

There are restaurants to suit all tastes and budgets in Washington. On this page they are listed by cuisine. For a more detailed description of each restaurant, see Washington by Area.

AMERICAN

Equinox (▷ 31)
Georgia Brown's (▷ 31)
Grapeseed (▷ 106)
Inn at Little Washington (▷ 106)
Komi (▷ 93)
Mitsitam Café (▷ 52)
Nora (▷ 94)
Palena (▷ 94)
Restaurant Eve (▷ 106)
Zola (▷ 32)

ASIAN

CityZen (▷ 52)
Mie N Yu (▷ 80)
Pho 75 (▷ 106)
Singapore Bistro (▷ 32)
Sushi Taro (▷ 94)
Teaism (▷ 94)
Ten Penh (▷ 32)
Thai Chef (▷ 94)

BURGERS

Ben's Chili Bowl (▷ 93)
Five Guys (▷ 31, 80)

FRENCH

Bistro Bis (▷ 68)
Café Bonaparte (▷ 80)
Central Michel Richard (▷ 31)
Michel Richard Citronelle (▷ 80)
Montmartre (▷ 68)

INDIAN

The Bombay Club (▷ 31)
Indique (▷ 93)
Nirvana (▷ 32)

ITALIAN

Maestro (▷ 106)
Matchbox (▷ 32)
Pizzeria Paradiso (▷ 80)
Ristorante Tosca (▷ 32)

LATIN

Banana Café and Piano Bar (▷ 68)
Café Atlantico (▷ 31)

MEDITERRANEAN

Jaleo (▷ 31)
Lebanese Taverna (▷ 94)
Mezè (▷ 94)
Neyla (▷ 80)
Zaytinya (▷ 32)

MEXICAN

Lauriol Plaza (▷ 93)
La Loma (▷ 68)
Oyamel (▷ 32)
Rosa Mexicano (▷ 32)
Taqueria Nacionale (▷ 68)
Well-Dressed Burrito (▷ 94)

MISCELLANEOUS

Amsterdam Falafelshop (▷ 93)
Belga Café (▷ 68)
Bukom Café (▷ 93)
Busboys and Poets (▷ 93)
The Diner (▷ 93)
Leopold's Kafe and Konditorei (▷ 80)
Madjet (▷ 94)
Marrakesh (▷ 32)

PICNICS, SOUPS & SANDWICHES

Breadline (▷ 31)
Dean and Deluca (▷ 80)
Firehook (▷ 68)
Marvelous Market (▷ 94)
Pavilion Café (▷ 52)

SEAFOOD

1789 (▷ 80)
Dr. Granville Moore's (▷ 106)
Hank's Oyster Bar (▷ 93)
Inn at 202 Dover (▷ 106)
Market Lunch (▷ 68)

STEAK

Charlie Palmer Steak (▷ 68)
Caucus Room (▷ 31)
Ray's the Steaks (▷ 106)

If You Like...

However you'd like to spend your time in Washington, these suggestions should help you tailor your ideal visit. Each suggestion has a fuller write-up elsewhere in the book.

A BIRD'S-EYE VIEW

Look over Downtown, the Capitol (▷ 60) and the Mall from the 270ft (82m) observation deck of the Old Post Office Building Tower (▷ 50).
Sip cocktails at the rooftop bar of the W Hotel (▷ 27) with a magnificent view of the Washington Monument.
Enjoy the 360-degree panorama over the Potomac and Foggy Bottom from the John F. Kennedy Center's (▷ 74) terraces.

TRAIPSING AROUND TOWN IN FANCY SHOES

Peruse Hu's Shoes' (▷ 77) unparalleled selection of high-end women's footwear.
Stroll out of Carbon (▷ 90), a U Street hotspot with hipster treads for men or women.
Don't pay a fortune for a trendy pair of shoes, go to Filene's Basement (▷ 29) for some real bargains.

*The Capitol (above);
Hu's Shoes (below);
Willard Intercontinental
Hotel (bottom)*

DINING OUT OF THE BOX

Sample 30 off-the-wall courses at José Andrés' Mini-Bar at Café Atlantico (▷ 31).
Enjoy the fresh flavors at Nora (▷ 94), America's first "organic" restaurant.

PASSING HOTSHOTS IN THE LOBBY

Sit by the fire in the Ritz-Carlton (▷ 112) but play it cool passing ambassadors, politicos and sheiks.
Soak up the history in the ornate lobby of the Willard Intercontinental (▷ 112), a short walk from the White House.

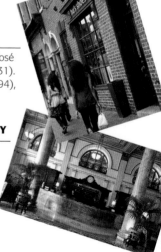

Spa pampering (below) and classical music at the Kennedy Center

BEING PAMPERED

Soak up the shaving lather and Musk in the plush Grooming Lounge (▷ 29).

Get the full treatment at the soothing spa in the Mandarin Oriental (▷ 112).

Enjoy the "wellness"-themed rooms, morning smoothies and yoga channel at Topaz Hotel (▷ 111), located in Dupont.

WATCHING WORLD-CLASS THEATER

Enjoy superbly acted and staged plays by Shakespeare and his peers at the Shakespeare Theatre (▷ 30).

Catch the world's best touring acts—from theater to music to dance—at the regal John F. Kennedy Center (▷ 74).

Go back in time and glimpse the avant garde at the home of the Woolly Mammoth Theater Company (▷ 30), DC's Steppenwolf.

KEEPING MONEY IN YOUR POCKET

Peruse the Smithsonian's free locations, from the National Zoological Park (▷ 84) to the National Air and Space Museum (▷ 40–41) to the National Gallery of Art (▷ 43).

Explore the almost 2,000 acres (810ha) of Rock Creek Park's (▷ 86) recreational space.

Rock Creek cyclists (above); fine wines on offer at Washington's bars (below)

A GREAT SELECTION AT THE BAR

Sip one of the bartenders' expert recommendations at Sonoma Wine Bar (▷ 67).

Wet your whistle with the world's best beers at Birreria Paradiso (▷ 78).

Try a pint of Belgium's finest at Belga Café (▷ 68).

KEEPING YOUR KIDS OCCUPIED

Entertaining the kids (below)

Let them play among America's flying machines at the National Air and Space Museum (▷ 40).

Discover the history of America's original inhabitants in the National Museum of the American Indian (▷ 44).

Wander amid the National Museum of Natural History's (▷ 50) dinosaur bones.

Let the Smithsonian Discovery Theater (▷ 49) dazzle with puppet shows, music and storytelling.

EATING WHERE LOCALS EAT

Slather your selection in beans and beef at this late-night institution: Ben's Chili Bowl (▷ 93).

Sip a frozen margarita on Lauriol Plaza's (▷ 93) roof deck amid young Hill staffers.

GETTING OUTDOORS

Follow the towpath along the Chesapeake & Ohio (C&O) Canal (▷ 75), through the forest from Georgetown to Maryland.

Wander among trees from almost every state at the National Arboretum (▷ 102).

Enjoy the verdant Bishop's Garden (▷ 87) in the shadow of the National Cathedral (▷ 88).

Ben's Chili Bowl (above middle); not just trees at the National Arboretum (above)

SHOPPING WITH THE CHIC SET

Smell the flowers, sample the cheese and sip a cappuccino at Dean and Deluca (▷ 80) amid Georgetowners shopping for gourmet treats.

Check out Balinese or Filipino home furnishings in the gorgeous showroom that is Muléh (▷ 91) on the up-and-coming 14th Street.

The popular Dean and Deluca in Georgetown (right)

This area, stretching from Chinatown east to the White House, has boomed in the last few years and is the city's nerve center. The district is especially popular at night.

3

4

NEW HAMPSHIRE AVENUE

CONNECTICUT

MASSACHUSETTS **AVENUE**

RHODE

ISLAND

AVENUE

O Street

Scott Circle

N Street

Thomas Circle

13TH STREET

N Street

Jefferson Place

St Matthews Cathedral

Jewish Museum

M STREET

M Street

DeSales Street

Explorers Hall

National Geographic Society

Metropolitan African Methodist Episcopal Church

Vermont

14TH STREET

L Street

L Street

K STREET

Farragut North

16th

15th

DOWNTOWN

20th

19th

18th

17th

Farragut West

St Johns Church

McPherson Square

Franklin Park

K Street

NEW YORK

13TH STREET

PENNSYLVANIA **AVENUE**

5

Renwick Gallery

H STREET

15th

14th

Chases Theater

H Street

W Hotel POV Roof Terrace

G Street

The White House

F Street

E STREET

Corcoran Gallery of Art

Warner Theater

National Theater

E STREET

19th

18th

D Street

DAR Museum

The Ellipse

VIRGINIA **AVENUE**

6

7

0 ___ 250 m
0 ___ 250 yds

E   **F**   **G**

National Geographic Society

National Geographic Society building (left); brass plate displayed in the Explorer's Hall (right)

THE BASICS

www.nationalgeographic.com/museum

✚ F4

✉ 1145 17th Street NW

☎ 202/857–7588

🕐 Mon–Sat 9–5, Sun 10–5

💵 Free for most exhibits

♿ Excellent

🚇 Farragut West, Farragut North

❓ Free showings of National Geographic specials in the TV room

HIGHLIGHTS

● The photography displays
● Accompanying cultural festivals

Best known as the entity that produces the *National Geographic Magazine*, the Society also breathes life into splendid exhibits at its headquarters by highlighting the work of its talented photographers.

Building the Society The Society was formed in 1888 and was soon after led by Alexander Graham Bell (1847–1922), the inventor of the telegraph. Bell picked Gilbert Hovey Grosvenor to head the magazine, and Grosvenor chose Bell's daughter to be his bride. Grosvenor transformed the magazine into "a vehicle for carrying the living, breathing, human interest truth about this great world of ours" by introducing stunning photography to its pages, a shocking idea at the time. In 1902, the original Beaux Arts building was constructed at the Society's current location. In 1964, a 10-floor tower designed by Kennedy Center architect Edward Durrell Stone was added. In 1984, this tour of 20th-century American architecture was completed with an angular terraced ziggurat.

Life in color Exhibits in Explorer's Hall, on the first floor of the Society's glass-and-marble building, change regularly and cover topics relating to nature, geography, exploration and the environment. One such display focused on aerial views of some 14 countries stretching from Mexico to Argentina. Exhibits often feature a festival in tandem. In October the Hall hosts the All Roads Film Project, featuring films from indigenous and under-represented cultures.

The White House

1600 Pennsylvania Avenue, the White House, first occupied by John Adams in 1800

THE BASICS

www.whitehouse.gov

➕ F5

✉ 1600 Pennsylvania Avenue

☎ 202/456–7041

🕐 Tue–Sat 7.30am–12.30pm

✋ Free

♿ Excellent

🚇 McPherson Square, Metro Center

❓ Requests for a free tour of the White house must be submitted via a Member of Congress and are accepted up to six months in advance. Citizens of foreign countries should contact their embassy in Washington for help in submitting a tour request. For historical exhibits, go to the White House Visitors Center, 15th and E streets

🕐 Daily 7.30–4

In the city's oldest public building, virtually every desk, every sterling tea service, every silver platter, decanter, painting and floor has witnessed historic events of the American democracy.

"The President's Palace" When he became the second occupant in 1800 of what was then known as the "President's Palace," Thomas Jefferson (1743–1826) thought James Hoban's (1762–1831) original design "big enough for two emperors, one Pope, and the grand Lama." Since then the building has undergone several renovations. The first was necessary after the British burned it in 1814. An almost complete renovation occurred during the Truman Administration (1945–53) after a piano broke through the floor, and an engineer determined that the building was staying erect only out of "force of habit."

Works of art The president's house holds an impressive display of decorative arts from the Sheraton, French and American Empire, Queen Anne and Federal periods. There are carved Carrara marble mantels, Bohemian cut-glass chandeliers and Turkish Hereke carpets. The tour may vary depending on official functions, but usually open are the ceremonial East Room, with Gilbert Stuart's 1797 *George Washington* portrait, the Vermeil Room containing 17th- and early 18th-century French and English gilded silver (vermeil), the small drawing, or Green, room, and the neoclassical State Dining Room where George P. A. Healy's (1808–94) *Abraham Lincoln* portrait hangs.

HIGHLIGHTS

● *Abraham Lincoln*, George P. A. Healy
● Jacqueline Kennedy's Rose Garden
● French and English gilded silver
● East Room
● *George Washington*, Gilbert Stuart

More to See

CORCORAN GALLERY OF ART

www.corcoran.org

Best known for its impressive collection of 19th- and 20th-century American art, the Corcoran also owns its fair share of European masterpieces.

➕ F6 ✉ 500 17th Street NW
☎ 202/639–1700 🕐 Wed, Fri–Sun 10–5, Thu 10–9 🚇 Farragut North, Farragut West
✋ Moderate; under 12 free

DAR MUSEUM

www.dar.org/museum

The National Society of the Daughters of the American Revolution has been collecting pre-Civil War, American artifacts for more than 100 years.

➕ F6 ✉ 1776 D Street NW ☎ 202/628–1776 🕐 Mon–Fri 9.30–4, Sat 9–5 🚇 Farragut West, Farragut North ✋ Moderate

INTERNATIONAL SPY MUSEUM

www.spymuseum.org

This child-friendly museum has the largest collection of spying artifacts ever put on display. Interactive exhibits highlight a detailed history of spying, techniques in the art of espionage and the latest spying trends.

➕ H5 ✉ 800 F Street NW ☎ 202/393–77988 🕐 Apr–end Aug 9–7; Sep–end Mar 10–6 🚇 Gallery Place–Chinatown
✋ Expensive

METROPOLITAN AFRICAN METHODIST EPISCOPAL CHURCH (AME)

www.metropolitanamec.org

The pulpit of this Gothic church, the "national cathedral" of the AME movement, has been used by Frederick Douglass, Martin Luther King Jr. and Winnie Mandela, among others, to speak against racial inequality.

➕ F4 ✉ 1518 M Street NW ☎ 202/331–1426 🕐 Mon–Sat 10–6 (but call ahead to check) 🚇 Farragut North

NATIONAL BUILDING MUSEUM

www.nbm.org

The dramatic interior of this building, punctuated by eight 75ft-tall (23m) Corinthian columns, houses exhibits on DC's cityscape, urban planning and architecture in general.

➕ H5 ✉ 401 F Street NW

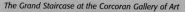
The Grand Staircase at the Corcoran Gallery of Art

☎ 202/272-2448 ⏰ Mon–Sat 10–5, Sun 11–5 🚇 Judiciary Square 💰 Free

NATIONAL PORTRAIT GALLERY

www.npg.si.edu

This renovated neoclassical gallery has portraits of famous Americans crafted by other famous Americans.

➕ H5 ✉ 8th and F streets NW
☎ 202/633-8300 ⏰ Daily 11.30–7
🚇 Gallery Place–Chinatown 💰 Free

NEWSEUM

www.newseum.org

This 250,000 sq ft (23,226 sq m) monument to the First Amendment reopened in 2008 with 14 state-of-the-art galleries that track the history and highlight the power of media.

➕ H6 ✉ Pennsylvania Avenue and 6th Street NW ☎ 888/639-7386 ⏰ Daily 9–5
🚇 Archive–Navy Memorial 💰 Expensive

RENWICK GALLERY

www.americanart.si.edu/renwick

Dedicated to American craft and decorative arts, the first floor hosts exceptional temporary exhibits.

➕ F5 ✉ 17th Street NW and Pennsylvania Avenue ☎ 202/633-2850 ⏰ Daily 10–5.30
🚇 Farragut North, Farragut West 💰 Free

SMITHSONIAN AMERICAN ART MUSEUM

www.americanart.si.edu

America's first national art collection has grown up to include works by John Singleton Copley, Georgia O'Keeffe, Edward Hopper and Thomas Cole.

➕ H5 ✉ 8th and F streets NW
☎ 202/633-7970 ⏰ Daily 11.30–7
🚇 Gallery Place–Chinatown 💰 Free

W HOTEL POV ROOF TERRACE

www.opentable.com

The ultra modern W Hotel has taken over this landmark building and made its famous roof terrace even more fabulous. Take in stunning vistas of the city's monuments while indulging in superb cocktails and tasty tapas.

➕ G5 ✉ 515 15th Street NW ☎ 202/631-2478 ⏰ Mon–Thu 11am–2am, Fri 11am–3am, noon–3am, Sun noon–2am
🚇 McPherson Square 💰 Expensive

Keep the kids entertained at the International Spy Museum

Presidential Route

A tour that passes many of the sites on the inaugural walk, finishing at the White House.

DISTANCE: 2.25 miles (3.6km) **ALLOW:** 2 hours 45 minutes

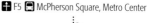

START

US CAPITOL (▷ 60–61)
🚩 J6 🚇 Union Station, Capitol South

① Begin on the west steps of the Capitol building (▷ 60–61). The view takes in Washington's famous museums and monuments, from the US Botanic Garden (▷ 58–59) and federal office buildings (left along Maryland Avenue), to the Washington Monument (▷ 46–47) and Lincoln Memorial (▷ 39) directly ahead, to the domes of the National Museum of Natural History (▷ 50) and the National Gallery of Art (▷ 43), on the right.

② Follow Pennsylvania Avenue past the I. M. Pei's East Building of the National Gallery of Art and on past the Newseum to the National Archives (▷ 42) and Navy Memorial.

③ Turn right onto 7th Street and follow it up through DC's quickly gentrifying Chinatown to the National Portrait Gallery (▷ 27).

END

THE WHITE HOUSE (▷ 25)
🚩 F5 🚇 McPherson Square, Metro Center

⑦ Take a left onto Pennsylvania Avenue, which passes between Lafayette Park and the White House (▷ 25).

⑥ Turn right onto 15th Street, past the 1836 Treasury Building, which you might recognize from the $10 bill.

⑤ Continue south on 10th Street and then turn right onto Pennsylvania Avenue. The clock tower of the Old Post Office (▷ 50) across the intersection offers views of the city. Farther up Pennsylvania you will pass Freedom Plaza, with its stone map of L'Enfant's city plan, and Pershing Park.

④ Head west along G Street and then turn left on 10th Street. Two blocks south you will pass Ford's Theatre (▷ 30), where Abraham Lincoln was fatally wounded in 1865. The FBI Building is across E Street on the left.

WALK

DOWNTOWN

28

Shopping

AMERICAN APPAREL

This temple to the T-shirt and other simple cotton clothing draws a congregation of DC hipsters.

➕ G5 ✉ 1090 F Street NW
☎ 202/628-0438
🕐 Mon–Fri 10–9, Sat 10–9, Sun 12–7 Ⓜ Metro Center

ANN TAYLOR LOFT

This outlet store offers classic, elegant women's clothing, shoes and jewelry at sharp discounts.

➕ H5 ✉ 707 7th Street NW
☎ 202/628-1224
🕐 Mon–Sat 10–9, Sun 11–7
Ⓜ Gallery Place

BED BATH & BEYOND

This mega home store has everything you need including bedding, framed posters, candles, and kitchenware.

➕ H5 ✉ 709 7th Street NW
☎ 202/628-0002
🕐 Mon–Sat 9am–10pm, Sun 10–7 Ⓜ Gallery Place

COUP DE FOUDRE

"Love at First Sight" carries high-end European lingerie in its elegant boudoir.

➕ G6 ✉ Corner of 11th and E Street NW ☎ 202/393-0878
🕐 Mon–Sat 11–6 Ⓜ Federal Triangle

COWGIRL CREAMERY

The East-Coast outpost of the Point Reyes, California original, Cowgirl Creamery offers award-winning cheese, charcuterie, breads and beer and best quality wine.

➕ H5 ✉ 919 F Street NW
☎ 202/393-6880

🕐 Mon–Fri 7.30–7, Sat 11–7
Ⓜ Gallery–Chinatown

FAHRNEY'S PENS

This 77-year-old institution stocks traditional and cutting-edge pens and stationery.

➕ G5 ✉ 1317 F Street NW
☎ 202/628-9525 🕐 Mon–Fri 9–5.30, Sat 10–5 Ⓜ Metro Center

FILENE'S BASEMENT

This huge bargain basement is packed with men's and women's clothing, shoes and accessories, all with designer labels.

➕ G5 ✉ 529 14th Street NW ☎ 202/638-4100
🕐 Mon–Sat 9.30–8, Sun 12–5
Ⓜ Metro Center

GALLERY PLACE

Part of the new Downtown revival, the Gallery Place complex has a movie theater, a bowling alley and retailers like Aveda, Ann Taylor and Urban Outfitters.

➕ H5 ✉ 7th and H streets NW 🕐 Hours vary
Ⓜ Gallery Place–Chinatown

BASIC NEEDS

Stranger in a strange land? Radio Shack sells voltage converters (732 7th Street NW and other locations, 202/638-5689). Fortuna Shoe and Luggage Repair will fix your bags or treads (1204 G Street NW, 202/347-4419). For all other needs, head to the DC Visitor Information Center (▷ 122).

GROOMING LOUNGE

Carrying fine grooming and shaving products, the Lounge pampers the modern male with shoe shines, shaves, haircuts, and pedicures.

➕ F4 ✉ 1745 L Street NW
☎ 202/466-8900
🕐 Mon–Fri 9–7, Sat 9–6, Sun 10–5 Ⓜ Farragut North, Farragut West

J. PRESS

Opened at Yale University in 1902, this traditional clothier still strives to "dress men to the Ivy League standard."

➕ F4 ✉ 1801 L Street NW
☎ 202/857-0120
🕐 Mon–Sat 9.30–6
Ⓜ Farragut North, Farragut West

MUSIC BOX CENTER

This quirky music box repository currently has more than 1,500 in stock, including those that play "What a Wonderful World" and "Up Where We Belong."

➕ E5 ✉ 1920 I Street NW
☎ 202/783-9399
🕐 Sun–Fri 10–5, Sat 10–3
Ⓜ Farragut West

REITER'S BOOKS

Washington's oldest independent bookstore features scientific, technical and professional titles, plus puzzles, games and toys for children of all ages.

➕ E4–5 ✉ 1990 K Street NW
☎ 800/537-4314 🕐 Mon–Thu 9–8, Fri 9–7, Sat 10–6, Sun 12–5 Ⓜ Farragut West

Entertainment and Nightlife

DAR CONSTITUTION HALL

www.stubhub.com

This 3,700-seat hall hosts musical performances, staged shows and some big-name comedy acts.

🚇 F6 ✉ 1776 D Street NW ☎ 202/638-2661 🚇 Farragut West, then walk six blocks south

FORD'S THEATER

Looking much as it did when Abraham Lincoln was shot here, Ford's now mainly hosts musicals, many with family appeal.

🚇 G5 ✉ 511 10th Street NW ☎ 202/347-4833 🚇 Metro Center

INDEBLEU

www.indebleu.com

This modern bar serves hip cocktails off its distinctive Metro-map menu.

🚇 H5 ✉ 707 G Street NW ☎ 202/333-2538 🕐 Sun–Thu 5pm-1.30am, Fri–Sat 5pm-2.30am 🚇 Gallery Place–Chinatown

NATIONAL THEATRE

www.nationaltheatre.org

The National Theater, operating in the same location since 1835, presents pre- and post-Broadway shows.

🚇 G6 ✉ 1321 Pennsylvania Avenue NW ☎ 202/628-6161 🚇 Metro Center

POSTE

www.postebrasserie.com

Poste's huge courtyard patio at the Hotel Monaco mixes well with the bartender's tasty seasonal alcohol infusions.

🚇 H5 ✉ 555 8th Street NW ☎ 202/783-6060 🍸 Bar hours: daily 11.30am–midnight 🚇 Gallery Place–Chinatown

RFD

Despite its cavernous space, RFD is frequently packed, drawing patrons with a lively atmosphere and encyclopedic beer list.

🚇 H5 ✉ 810 7th Street NW ☎ 202/289-2030 🕐 Mon–Thu 11am-1.30am, Fri–Sat 11am-2.30am, Sun noon-12.30am 🚇 Gallery Place–Chinatown

ROUND ROBIN

This circular, mahogany bar maintains the same atmosphere that it did in the early 19th century when Senator Henry Clay introduced the bartender, and DC, to the mint julep.

🚇 G6 ✉ 1401 Pennsylvania Avenue NW ☎ 202/628-9100 🕐 Mon–Thu 4.30pm-1am, Fri 3pm-1am, Sat noon-1am 🚇 Metro Center

WHERE THE ACTION IS

Screen on the Green

On Monday nights throughout July and August the Mall is turned into a free open-air cinema screening classic films, ranging from Elvis Presley musicals to Hitchcock's thrillers. Washingtonians arrive as early as 5pm to save a spot, make new friends and picnic on the lawn stretching west from 7th Street.

SCIENCE CLUB

www.scienceclubdc.com

A narrow, multistory lounge with chic decor, a veg-friendly menu and DJs in the back room. Different music types—check for your favorites.

🚇 E4 ✉ 1136 19th Street NW ☎ 202/775-0747 🕐 Mon–Thu 5pm-2am, Fri–Sat 5pm-3am 🚇 Farragut North

SHAKESPEARE THEATRE

www.shakespearetheatre.org

This acclaimed troupe, known as one of the world's three great Shakespearean companies, crafts fantastically staged and acted performances of works by the Bard and his contemporaries.

🚇 H6 ✉ 450 7th Street NW ☎ 877/487-8849 🚇 Gallery Place–Chinatown

VERIZON CENTER

www.verizoncenter.com

The 20,000-seat home of Washington's pro basketball and hockey teams also hosts DC's biggest concerts and the circus.

🚇 H5 ✉ 601 F Street NW ☎ 202/628-3200 🚇 Gallery Place–Chinatown

WOOLLY MAMMOTH THEATRE COMPANY

www.woollymammoth.net

This resident group presents unusual, avant-garde shows in its modern space.

🚇 H6 ✉ 641 D Street NW ☎ 202/393-3939 🚇 Gallery Place–Chinatown

Restaurants

THE BOMBAY CLUB ($$–$$$)
www.bombayclubdc.com
A block from the White House, this beautiful Indian restaurant emulates a private British club in 19th-century India.
🔲 F5 ⊠ 815 Connecticut Avenue NW ☎ 202/659–3727 🅒 Mon–Fri lunch, dinner; Sat dinner; Sun 5.30–9 🔲 Farragut West

BREADLINE ($)
This one-of-a-kind bakery-café, a favorite among White House staff, turns out warm rolls, a variety of sandwiches and homemade soups.
🔲 F5 ⊠ 1751 Pennsylvania Avenue NW ☎ 202/822–8900 🅒 Mon–Fri 7.30–3.30 🔲 Farragut West

CAFÉ ATLANTICO ($$–$$$)
www.cafeatlantico.com
This brainchild of the celebrity chef José Andrés serves delicious pan-South American food. At Minibar the 30-course tasting menu offers up tasty bite-size portions.
🔲 H6 ⊠ 405 8th Street NW ☎ 202/393–0812 🅒 Tue–Sat lunch, dinner; Sun dinner only 🔲 Gallery Place–Chinatown

CAUCUS ROOM ($$–$$$)
www.thecaucusroom.com
This clubby steak parlor is where the powerful talk politics over rib-eyes and creamed spinach.
🔲 H6 ⊠ 401 9th Street NW ☎ 202/393–1300 🅒 Mon–Fri lunch; Mon–Sat dinner 🔲 Archives–Navy Memorial

CENTRAL MICHEL RICHARD ($$)
www.centralmichelrichard.com
Michel Richard's second DC effort, offering a similar slate of French-styled American classics, is as well executed as his first (Citronelle). And it's more affordable.
🔲 G6 ⊠ 1001 Pennsylvania Avenue NW ☎ 202/626–0015 🅒 Mon–Fri lunch, dinner; Sat–Sun dinner 🔲 Metro Center

COFFEE CULTURE
To accommodate DC's hard-working Hill staff and think tankers who often have to work nights and weekends, this city is packed with superb places to grab some coffee and clack away on your laptop. The following independent cafés have great coffee and free wireless: Tryst (2459 18th Street NW; 202/232–5500; no wireless on weekends), Love Café (1501 U Street NW; 202/265–9800), Busboys and Poets (2021 14th Street; 202/387–7638) and Murky Coffee (660 Pennsylvania Avenue NW; 202/546–5228).

EQUINOX ($$$)
www.equinoxrestaurant.com
Chef Todd Gray uses seasonal ingredients to build beautiful and traditional regional dishes, including panfried Chesapeake oysters and bacon-wrapped Cervena venison medallions. Dinner is 3-, 4- or 6-course tasting menu. Reservations requested.
🔲 F5 ⊠ 818 Connecticut Avenue NW ☎ 202/331–8118 🅒 Mon–Fri lunch; daily dinner 🔲 Farragut West

FIVE GUYS ($)
www.fiveguys.com
This no-nonsense joint prides itself on using fine ingredients, fresh ground beef and peanut oil in its burgers and fries.
🔲 H5 ⊠ 808 H Street NW ☎ 202/393–2900 🅒 Daily lunch, dinner 🔲 Gallery Place–Chinatown

GEORGIA BROWN'S ($$)
www.gbrowns.com
This elegant restaurant attracts government officials and journalists with its southern specials.
🔲 F5 ⊠ 950 15th Street NW ☎ 202/393–4499 🅒 Mon–Fri lunch, dinner; Sat dinner; Sun brunch, dinner 🔲 McPherson Square

JALEO ($$)
www.jaleo.com
A lively tapas restaurant, José Andrés' Jaleo serves up small plates that cater to any craving, whether it be for homemade chorizo or fried squid with alioli.

🏠 H6 ✉ 480 7th Street NW
☎ 202/628–7949 🕐 Daily
lunch, dinner 🚇 Gallery
Place–Chinatown

MARRAKESH ($$)

www.marrakesh.us
Stepping into this
Moroccan restaurant,
on a block of auto repair
shops, is like stepping into
another world. Groups
share fixed-price feasts
amid photos of famous
customers and a nightly
show of belly dancers.
🏠 H5 ✉ 617 New York
Avenue NW ☎ 202/393–
9393 🕐 Daily dinner
🚇 Mount Vernon Square

MATCHBOX ($$)

www.matchboxdc.com
This warm, stylish pizzeria
impresses with wood-
oven, gourmet pies and
miniburgers, plus a pleasant deck with a fireplace.
🏠 H5 ✉ 713 H Street NW
☎ 202/289–4441
🕐 Daily lunch, dinner
🚇 Gallery Place–Chinatown

NIRVANA ($)

www.dcnirvana.com
Specializing in vegetarian
Indian cuisine, Nirvana
offers a daily lunch buffet
highlighting a different
Indian region.
🏠 F5 ✉ 1810 K Street NW
☎ 202/223–5043 🕐 Mon–
Sat lunch, dinner 🚇 Farragut
North, Farragut West

OYAMEL ($–$$)

www.oyamel.com
José Andrés solidified his
grip on Downtown when
his fourth restaurant

opened in 2007. Oyamel
sports some of the best
cocktails in town, solid
Oaxacan cuisine and a
live, projected view of a
Mexican market.
🏠 H6 ✉ 401 7th Street NW
☎ 202/628–1005 🕐 Daily
lunch, dinner 🚇 Gallery
Place–Chinatown

RISTORANTE TOSCA ($$$)

www.toscadc.com
Northern Italian
specialties are cooked to
perfection in this comfortable, beige dining room.
🏠 G5 ✉ 1112 F Street NW
☎ 202/367–1990
🕐 Mon–Sat lunch, dinner
🚇 Metro Center

ROSA MEXICANO ($$)

www.rosamexicano.com
Dominated by a rich blue
tile wall, Rosa Mexicano
specializes in pomegran-
ate margaritas and
high-end Mexican food.

RESTAURANT WEEK

For a full week each January
and August, a host of
Washington DC's restaurants,
including some of its finest,
offer three-course, fixed-price
lunch menus for around $20
and dinner menus for
around $30. Some restau-
rants only offer a limited
selection and others only
offer lunch or dinner, not
both. Make reservations well
in advance.
www.washington.org/
restaurantwk

🏠 H5 ✉ 575 7th Street NW
☎ 202/783–5522
🕐 Daily lunch, dinner
🚇 Gallery Place–Chinatown

SINGAPORE BISTRO ($)

www.singaporebistro.com
This skinny town house
serves high-grade sushi
and some of the best
pan-Asian food in town.
🏠 E4 ✉ 1134 19th Street
NW ☎ 202/659–2660
🕐 Mon–Sat lunch, dinner;
Sun dinner 🚇 Farragut North

TEN PENH ($$)

www.tenpenh.com
This is a hip scene with
Asian fusion cuisine.
🏠 G6 ✉ 1001 Pennsylvania
Avenue NW ☎ 202/393–
4500 🕐 Mon–Fri lunch,
dinner; Sat, Sun dinner
🚇 Federal Triangle

ZAYTINYA ($$)

www.zaytinya.com
This light and airy
Mediterranean *meze*
spot is popular for its
inventive cuisine and
modern scene.
🏠 H5 ✉ 701 9th Street NW
☎ 202/638–0800
🕐 Daily lunch, dinner
🚇 Gallery Place–Chinatown

ZOLA ($$)

www.zoladc.com
Chef Frank Morales'
upscale version of classic
American cuisine is to
die for.
🏠 H5 ✉ 800 F Street NW
☎ 202/654–0999
🕐 Mon–Fri lunch, dinner;
Sat–Sun dinner 🚇 Gallery
Place–Chinatown

The mile-long stretch of grass from the Capitol to the Washington Monument.

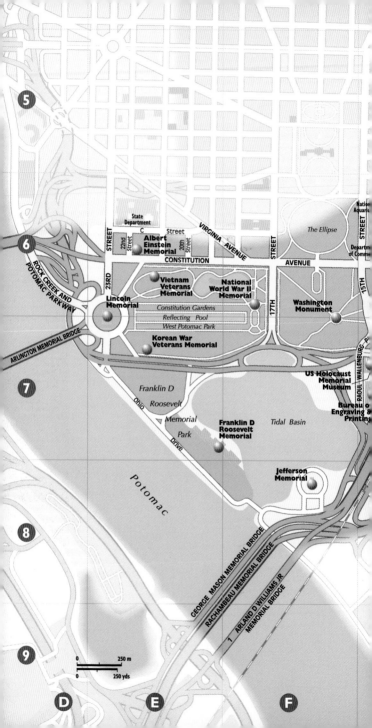

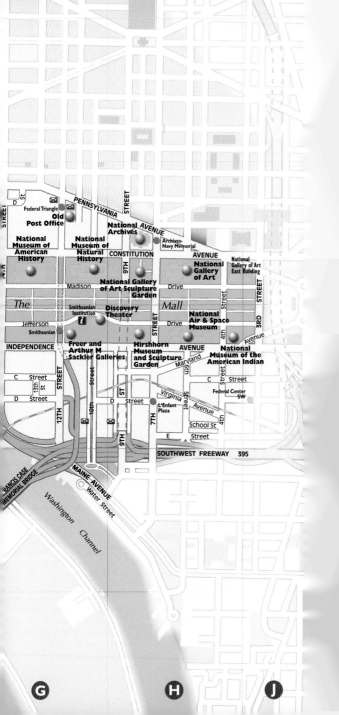

The Tidal Basin (right);
bronze statue of
Thomas Jefferson
(left); the Jefferson
Memorial (opposite)

FDR and Jefferson Memorials

The Jefferson Memorial was dedicated by President Franklin Delano Roosevelt on the 200th anniversary of Jefferson's birth, April 13, 1943. Roosevelt's own memorial was created nearby and dedicated in 1997.

Classical The contributions of Thomas Jefferson, a brilliant and eloquent statesman and America's third president, are commemorated in a white-marble, neoclassical memorial set along Washington's Tidal Basin amid 3,700 Japanese cherry trees. The Memorial was modeled by architect John Pope (1874–1937) on buildings that Jefferson had designed himself at his own home and the University of Virginia, which, in turn, showed deference to the Pantheon in Rome. The open interior of the building contains a 19ft (5.8m) bronze of Jefferson, circled by excerpts of Jefferson's speeches and writings inscribed into the walls. An inscription above Jefferson reads, "I have sworn upon the altar of God eternal hostility against every form of tyranny over the mind of man."

Sculpture Franklin Delano Roosevelt (1882–1945), America's president from the Great Depression through the end of World War II, is memorialized by a sprawling park on the west side of the Tidal Basin. The Memorial, cloaked in shady trees amid waterfalls and quiet pools, is divided into four outdoor "rooms," each commemorating one of FDR's four terms in office, by far the most of any president. Nine sets of bronze sculptures, one of which is a controversial depiction of FDR in a wheelchair, punctuate the park.

THE BASICS

Jefferson Memorial
www.nps.gov/thje
F8
Tidal Basin, south bank
202/426–6841
Daily 24 hours.
Rangers available to answer questions daily 9.30–1.30
Free Excellent
Smithsonian, then 15-min walk

FDR Memorial
www.nps.gov/fdrm
E7
West Potomac Park, Tidal Basin, west bank
202/426–6841
As for Jefferson above
Free Smithsonian, then 10–15 min walk

HIGHLIGHTS

- Jefferson bronze
- Inscribed Declaration of Independence
- Wheelchair statue of FDR
- Surrounding cherry trees
- Boat rides in the Tidal Basin

THE MALL

TOP 25

Freer and Arthur M. Sackler Galleries

The central fountain in the impressive courtyard at the Freer Gallery

THE BASICS

www.asia.si.edu

G7

12th Street and Jefferson Drive (Freer) 1050 Independence Avenue SW (Sackler)

202/633–4880

Daily 10–5.30

Free

Excellent

Smithsonian

Tours daily. The Sackler is connected to the Freer via an underground passage

HIGHLIGHTS

The Freer Gallery of Art
● *The Peacock Room*, James McNeill Whistler
● *Princess from the Land of Porcelain*, James McNeill Whistler
● Ancient Chinese artifacts
● Korean ceramics
● Japanese painted screens

The Arthur M. Sackler Gallery
● Chinese jades and bronzes
● Islamic manuscripts
● Ancient Iranian metalworks

One of the lesser known treasures of the city, the Freer and Sackler galleries contain more than 26,000 works of Asian art, as well as one of the world's largest collections of paintings by James McNeill Whistler (1834–1903).

Freer Gallery of Art Housed in a granite palazzo-style building, designed by "American Renaissance" architect Charles A. Platt (1861–1933), the Freer houses a wide range of art including Asian porcelains, Japanese screens, Chinese painting and bronzes, Korean stoneware and Islamic art. *The Peacock Room*, painted in blue and gold designs by Whistler, was once part of a London town house. The owner was away when Whistler used his fine leather walls as a canvas, and sparked an ongoing fued between the two. Freer Gallery founder, Charles Lang Freer (1854–1919), purchased the room, which was installed in his Detroit home before being moved here after his death.

Arthur M. Sackler Gallery A beautifully constructed, subterranean museum, the Sackler contains its own impressive collection of Asian art, including ceramics, printing, metalwork, bronzes and jades. More than 1,000 of these works were donated in 1987 by Arthur M. Sackler, a physician and publisher who subsequently gave $4 million for the construction of the building. Fantastic touring exhibits have recently brought portraits, Southeast Asian ceramics and ancient winemaking objects from Georgia to the Sackler. The Meyer Auditorium hosts Asian films, lectures, music and theater.

Lincoln Memorial

The Lincoln Memorial (left); sculpture of Lincoln (middle); Washington Monument (right)

So powerful and somber is this memorial that you could easily imagine Lincoln rising up and resuming his epic struggles. The view from the steps at sunset is one of the city's most romantic, with the Washington Monument reflected in the rectangular pool at its base.

Tribute Architect Henry Bacon (1866–1924) chose a Greek Doric style for Lincoln's memorial because he felt that a memorial to a man who had sacrificed so much to defend democracy should be modeled after the style found in the birthplace of democracy. Construction, during World War I, was not without difficulties. The site, a swamp, required the builders to dig down almost 65ft (19.8m) to find a suitable foundation. Almost 38,000 tons of material, mainly marble, was transported from locations as far away as Colorado. The statue of Lincoln was so large that it had to be constructed inside the Memorial.

History in stone Bacon's white marble temple to Lincoln contains Daniel Chester French's (1850–1931) 19ft (5.8m) seated statue of the president. It is estimated that, were Lincoln to stand up, he would be 28ft tall (8.5m). The statue's chamber is flanked by two smaller rooms, which contain inscriptions of Lincoln's Gettysburg and second inaugural addresses and two beautiful murals. The area surrounding the reflecting pool that stretches east from the foot of the monument has hosted seminal events in America's history, most notably Martin Luther King Jr.'s "I Have a Dream" speech.

THE BASICS

www.nps.gov/linc

🚇 E6

✉ 23rd Street NW between Constitution and Independence avenues (west end of the Mall)

☎ 202/426–6841

🕐 As for Jefferson (▷ 37)

💰 Free

♿ Excellent

🚇 Foggy Bottom

❓ Tours on request

HIGHLIGHTS

● Daniel Chester French's *Lincoln*
● Inscriptions of Lincoln's 1863 Gettysburg Address and Second Inaugural Address
● Reflecting pool
● View at sunset

National Air and Space Museum

HIGHLIGHTS

- Wright brothers' 1903 *Flyer*
- Charles Lindbergh's *Spirit of St. Louis*
- Chuck Yeager's *Bell X-1 Glamorous Glennis*
- The Steven F. Udvar-Hazy Center
- John Glenn's *Friendship* and *Apollo 11*
- *Columbia* Space Shuttle
- Skylab
- Lunar Exploration Vehicles

TIP

- Looking for smaller crowds? Take a shuttle to the hangars at the Udvar-Hazy Center, where you can also see an array of impressive flying machines.

The most visited museum on the Mall takes parents and children alike on a pioneering journey from the first manned motorized flight to the most recent space exploration—"infinity and beyond!"

Flight pioneers The Smithsonian's bicentennial gift to the nation, this museum receives almost 9 million visitors a year in its monumental glass-and-granite galleries. The collection—begun as early as 1861, when the first secretary of the Smithsonian urged experiments in balloon flight—includes the Wright brothers' 1903 *Flyer*; Charles Lindbergh's *Spirit of St. Louis*; Chuck Yeager's *Bell X-1*, in which he broke the sound barrier; and *The Voyager*, the plane in which Dick Rutan and Jeana Yeager flew nonstop around the world in 1986.

The Apollo lunar rover (left) and the space shuttle Enterprise *(right) at the National Air and Space Musuem*

Into space Visitors can touch a moon rock and see the Apollo 11 command module, Skylab and the *Columbia* Space Shuttle. Aside from the *Milestones of Flight*, this museum also houses exhibits on the half-century space race between the United States and the Soviet Union, exploring the planets of our solar system, the global positioning system and the science of flight, among many others. Visitors who tire of the museum's colossal collection can take in an IMAX film, go for a test run in a flight simulator, or visit the Albert Einstein Planetarium and tour the universe on the *Infinity Express*. Despite its enormity, this building can only hold about 10 percent of the Museum's collection. Most of the rest is housed in hangars at the Steven F. Udvar-Hazy Center at Dulles International Airport. A shuttle service between the two museums is available.

THE BASICS

www.nasm.si.edu
✚ H7
✉ Independence Avenue at 4th Street SW
☎ 202/633–1000 (same for Udvar-Hazy Center)
🕐 Daily 10–5.30
💲 Free. Albert Einstein Planetarium: moderate
♿ Excellent
🍴 Wright Place Food Court
Ⓜ L'Enfant Plaza, Smithsonian
❓ Lockhead Martin IMAX, Udvar-Hazy IMAX: call for schedules. Tours daily

National Archives

Visitors inspecting the Constitution, Declaration of Independence and Bill of Rights

THE BASICS

www.archives.gov/
H6
Constitution Avenue at 7th Street NW
202/357–5000
Daily 10–5.30; summer 10–7
Free
Excellent
Archives–Navy Memorial
Tours daily 10.15, 1.15 (reservations required)

HIGHLIGHTS

● Charters of Freedom
● Murals by Barry Faulkner
● Changing exhibition gallery

Behind this building's colossal bronze doors, America's story comes alive through millions of primary materials, including the founding documents, the rifle that shot John F. Kennedy (1917–63) and the Watergate tapes.

Charters of Freedom Under low light in the magnificent central rotunda lie 14 of America's founding documents, including the Constitution, the Declaration of Independence and the Bill of Rights. All have been encased in state-of-the-art, gold-plated, titanium frames filled with inert argon gas. Two recently restored 340lb (154.5kg) murals, *The Constitution* and *The Declaration of Independence*, accentuate the experience.

Archival splendor The Archives is most famous for the aforementioned Charters of Freedom, but this building contains billions of other documents, maps and photographs, along with hundreds of thousands of miles of film and videotapes, the most entertaining and instructional of which are on display in the "Public Vaults." This child-friendly area showcases audio recordings of congressional debates on prohibition, video clips of former Presidents cracking jokes and behind-the-scenes conversations between President Kennedy and his advisors during the Cuban Missile Crisis, among many other exhibits, all displayed in accessible multimedia presentations. The William G. McGowan Theater screens films about the Archives and the Charters of Freedom by day and documentary films at night.

Monet's **Woman with a Parasol** *(left); the Kogood Courtyard (right)*

National Gallery of Art

The two buildings of the Gallery, architectural wonders filled with serene spots to sit and reflect, are reason enough to visit, but they also house one of the world's most incredible art collections ranging from the Middle Ages to the modern day.

West Building Designed by John Pope in the Classical style, this building was funded by a gift from Andrew Mellon, a former Treasury Secretary. Mellon also donated an impressive collection of art that has been augmented to fill the building's many galleries. Of particular interest are da Vinci's *Ginevra*, works by Vermeer and Monet, and a comprehenisve collection of American art. The massive building is accentuated by a large rotunda filled with flowers and the gentle sounds of a fountain and by small garden courts in each wing of the building. The National Gallery frequently draws and creates some of the nation's finest temporary exhibits. The West Building recently displayed a large collection of landscapes by British artists.

East Building Connected to the West Building by an underground plaza, this architectural masterpiece was created by the designer of the Louvre Pyramid, I. M. Pei (1917–), and opened in 1978. The building's atrium contains a massive mobile designed by Alexander Calder (1898–1976). The galleries focus on 20th-century art, including the works of Henri Matisse, Andy Warhol, Pablo Picasso and Jackson Pollock. The East Building recently displayed America's first comprehensive collection of Edward Hopper's work ouside of New York in 25 years.

THE BASICS

www.nga.gov

H6

Entrances on the Mall, on 7th Street, Constitution Avenue, 6th Street and 4th Street

202/737–4215

Mon–Sat 10–5, Sun 11–6

Free

Excellent

Pavilion Café, Garden Café

Archives, Judiciary, Smithsonian

Tours daily

HIGHLIGHTS

● **East Wing**
● *Venus and Adonis*, Titian
● *The Alba Madonna*, Raphael
● *Laocoön*, El Greco
● *Daniel in the Lion's Den*, Peter Paul Rubens
● *Woman Holding a Balance*, Johannes Vermeer
● *A Girl with a Watering Can*, Auguste Renoir
● *Woman with a Parasol– Madame Monet and her Son*, Claude Monet
● *The Skater*, Gilbert Stuart

National Museum of the American Indian

The futuristic exterior (left); traditional shirt (middle); the rotunda display (right)

THE BASICS

www.nmai.si.edu

🕂 H7

✉ 4th Street SW and Independence Avenue

☎ 202/633–1000

🕐 Daily 10–5.30

💷 Free

♿ Excellent

Ⓜ L'Enfant Plaza

HIGHLIGHTS

● Limestone exterior and "grandfather rocks"
● Welcome Wall
● *Who We Are* video
● *A Thousand Roads* video
● *Wall of Gold*
● 20ft (6m) totem pole by Nathan Jackson
● Light-filled atrium
● Navajo weavings

The first national museum dedicated to Native Americans, this Smithsonian building manages to pay homage to thousands of cultures with great cohesion. Well designed throughout, its exhibits are light years beyond traditional anthropological displays.

Connection to nature   The newest addition to the Mall cuts a unique figure. The exterior, fashioned out of Minnesota limestone, resembles a weatherworn rock mass, and the building sits on a serene 4.25-acre (1.7ha) plot peppered with fountains and "grandfather rocks." Inside, light is refracted from a prism in the ceiling into the museum's five-floor "Potomac" atrium, which often plays host to traditonal ceremonies.

Break from tradition   The Museum breaks from the traditional anthropological treatment of Native Americans. *Our Universes* explores the spiritual relationship between humans and nature. *Our Peoples* documents the struggle to maintain a way of life in the face of adversity and aggression. The *Wall of Gold* displays hundreds of gold objects dating from the 15th century. And *Our Lives* examines the Native American identity and place in society today. The "Red Power" movement of the '60s and '70s is highlighted. A large gallery space showcases the talents of Native American artists. The circular Lelawi Theater offers a spectacular video, *Who We Are*. The Rasmuson Theater features the Museum's signature film, *A Thousands Roads*.

US Holocaust Memorial Museum

People visit the museum (left) to pay their respects at the displays (middle) and remember the lives lost (right)

This memorial to the 6 million people killed by the Nazis between 1933 and 1945 graphically portrays both the personal stories and the wider issues of persecution and human tragedy. The museum sets new standards for design and historical interpretation.

Disturbing "You cannot deal with the Holocaust as a reasonable thing," explained architect James Ingo Freed (1930–2005). To that end, he created a discordant building, intended to disturb the classical and sometimes placid facades elsewhere in Washington. Likewise, the central atrium, the Hall of Witness, disorients with twisted skylights, exposed load-bearing brick and architectural elements that don't join in conventional ways.

Nightmare The main exhibit doesn't pull any punches. Visitors are given identity cards that detail the life of a Holocaust victim as they enter a detailed history of the rise of anti-Semitism in Europe, the Nazi party and the machinations of the Holocaust. The brilliant and shocking displays are rendered using high-tech audiovisuals. Sometimes even the most stoic viewers are moved to tears. The Hall of Remembrance, a place for quiet reflection, is a welcome respite at the end of the experience. A special exhibit for children under 12, *Daniel's Story*, re-creates what life was like for a young boy trapped in the downward spiral of Nazi occupation. The Wexner Learning Center, which holds excellent temporary exhibitions, embodies the Museum's forward-looking efforts to curb genocide.

THE BASICS

www.ushmm.org

G7

☒ 14th Street and Wallenberg Place SW, south of Independence Avenue

☎ 202/488–0400

🕐 Daily 10–5.30. Closed Yom Kippur

💷 Free

♿ Excellent

🍴 Kosher restaurant

Ⓜ Smithsonian

❓ Free timed tickets distributed beginning at 9am; line up early (before 9am) or book 2 weeks in advance in spring or summer. See website for how to reserve tickets online

☎ 800/400–9373

HIGHLIGHTS

● Hall of Witness
● Hall of Remembrance
● For children (8–12): *Daniel's Story*

Washington Monument

HIGHLIGHTS

● Views from the top
● Exhibit in base

TIPS

● Make reservations online in advance, even during the off season.
● Take a map of the city with you to the top so that you can point out your favorite places.
● Try to go at sunset to see the whole city painted in pastels.

An icon of Washington life, this monolith is the world's tallest masonry structure. The 70-second ride to the top is rewarded with a marvelous panorama over DC, Maryland and Virginia.

Rogues and cattle The Washington National Monument Society was founded in 1833 to solicit designs and funding for a memorial to America's first president. Construction began in 1848 but stopped in 1854 for 20 years, in part because a rogue political party stole and destroyed a stone donated by the Pope. During this time, herds of Union cattle grazed on the grounds of the half-finished monument. A ring still betrays the slightly different marble that had to be used years later as construction began again amid the fervor surrounding the centennial of the American

Clockwise from far left: The "Stars and Stripes" flying in the breeze below the Washington Monument; view from the top of the Monument; the obelisk towering over the city of Washington; the Monument reflected in the Tidal Basin; the Washington Monument and the Lincoln Memorial at dusk

Revolution. In 1884, 36 years after the cornerstone was placed, a 7.5lb (3.4kg) aluminum point, at the time one of the world's most expensive metals, was placed on top of the 555ft (169m) monument, the tallest building in the world at that time.

View The observation deck, which opened in 2002, is 500ft (152m) above the ground. The views from the top cover most of Washington, as well as parts of Maryland and Virginia: look for the Tidal Basin, the Jefferson and Lincoln memorials, the White House, the US Capitol, the Library of Congress and the Smithsonian Institution. If you take the weekend guided walk down the monument's 898 steps you will see the commemorative plaques donated by states, masonic lodges, church groups and foreign countries.

THE BASICS

www.nps.gov/wamo

✚ F6

✉ The Mall at 15th Street NW

☎ 202/426–6841

🕐 Daily 9–4.45

♿ $1.50 service charge per ticket ♿ Excellent

🚇 Smithsonian

❓ Timed tickets distributed daily starting at 8.30am at the site and through NPRS (☎ 877/444–6777; www.recreation.gov)

Vietnam Veterans Memorial

HIGHLIGHTS

● Inscribed names
● Frederick Hart's sculptural group
● Glenna Goodacre's sculptural group
● The city reflected in the polished stone

Opinions on this starkly simple sculpture have been as divided as those on the conflict that it commemorates. Some see it as the most moving memorial in Washington, while others have called it the "black gash of shame." What isn't in doubt is its popularity; on most days there is an almost constant procession of visitors.

Simple reminder Yale University student Maya Ying Lin (1959–) was only 21 when she won the national design competition with a simple memorial—two triangular black granite walls, each 246ft (75m) long, set at a 125-degree angle and pointing toward the Washington Monument and Lincoln Memorial. The walls rise to 10ft (3m), seeming to overpower those who stand below. Names of heroes who made the ultimate sacrifice for their country are listed chronologically. Between 1959 and 1975 more than 58,000 were killed or reported missing in action.

A place to reflect The polished surface reflects sky, trees, nearby monuments and the faces of visitors searching for the names of loved ones. Each day National Park Service Rangers collect mementoes left near soldiers' names: letters, uniforms, military emblems, photographs. These tokens receive the same care as museum acquisitions. Some are on display at the American History Museum. In 1984 Frederick Hart's slightly larger-than-life sculpture of three soldiers was dedicated at the south entrance to the Wall.

More to See

ALBERT EINSTEIN MEMORIAL

This four-ton bronze of Albert Einstein, situated in a small, shaded elm grove at the National Academy of Sciences, is an ideal spot for a photo.

✚ E6 ✉ Constitution Avenue and 22nd Street NW ⊙ Free access via the sidewalk ⊚ Foggy Bottom/GWU and 15-min walk

BUREAU OF ENGRAVING AND PRINTING

www.moneyfactory.gov

Children and adults alike delight in watching powerful printing presses turn out more than $541 million a day.

✚ G7 ✉ 14 and C streets SW ☎ 866/874–2330 ⊙ Mon–Fri 9–10.45, 12.30–2 ⊚ Smithsonian ⊌ Free ❓ Free 45-min guided tours every 15 mins. Tickets required Mar–Aug. Line forms on 14th Street

DISCOVERY THEATER

www.discoverytheater.org

Smithsonian shows dazzle and educate. Puppetry, music and storytelling.

✚ G7 ✉ 1100 Jefferson Drive SW ☎ 200/633–8700 ⊙ Call for schedule ⊚ Smithsonian ⊌ Inexpensive

HIRSHHORN MUSEUM AND SCULPTURE GARDEN

www.hirshhorn.si.edu

This gallery showcases some first-rate contemporary and modern art, including works by Henri Matisse, Man Ray and Andy Warhol.

✚ H7 ✉ 7th Street and Independence Avenue ☎ 202/633–1000 ⊙ Daily 10–5.30, garden 7.30am–dusk ⊚ L'Enfant Plaza ⊌ Free

KOREAN WAR VETERANS MEMORIAL

www.nps.gov/kwm

Dedicated in 1995, this memorial depicts 19 life-size figures marching through rugged terrain toward an American flag. The faces of 2,400 servicemen are etched into a wall nearby.

✚ E7 ✉ Between Lincoln Memorial and Independence Avenue ☎ 202/426–6841 ⊙ Daily 24 hours ⊌ Free

NATIONAL GALLERY OF ART SCULPTURE GARDEN

www.nga.gov

Many works by Louise Bourgeois,

THE MALL

★

MORE TO SEE

The life-size figures of the Korean War Veterans Memorial

Mark di Suveroi, Roy Lichtenstein and other 20th-century sculptors can be enjoyed in this 6.5-acre (2.6ha) garden.

✚ H6 ✉ Between Constitution Avenue and National Mall, 7th and 9th streets NW ☎ 202/737–4215 ◷ Mon–Sat 10–5, Sun 11–6. Skating rink: winter daily 11–10 🍴 Pavilion Café 🚇 Archives 🎟 Free. Skating inexpensive

NATIONAL MUSEUM OF AMERICAN HISTORY
www.americanhistory.si.edu
From Seinfeld's "puffy shirt" to inaugural ballgowns of the First Ladies, this newly renovated museum is where you can find America's mementoes.

✚ G6 ✉ Constitution Avenue and 14th Street NW ☎ 202/633–1000 ◷ Daily 10–5.30 🚇 Smithsonian, Federal Triangle 🎟 Free ❓ Tours

NATIONAL MUSEUM OF NATURAL HISTORY
www.mnh.si.edu
Dinosaurs and the Hope Diamond fossils, millions of plant and animal specimens are all housed here.

✚ G6 ✉ Constitution Avenue and 10th Street NW ☎ 202/633–1000 ◷ Daily 10–5.30 🚇 Smithsonian, Federal Triangle 🎟 Free

NATIONAL WORLD WAR II MEMORIAL
www.nps.gov/nwwm
Set on the axis between the Washington Monument and the Lincoln Memorial, this oval memorial commemorates the sacrifices made by Americans during World War II.

✚ F6 ✉ The Mall at 17th Street SW ☎ 202/619–7222 ◷ Daily 24 hours 🚇 Smithsonian, then 10-min walk 🎟 Free

OLD POST OFFICE BUILDING TOWER
www.oldpostofficedc.com
The clock tower here offers a dramatic view of the city.

✚ G6 ✉ Pennsylvania Avenue at 12th Street NW ☎ 202/606–8691 ◷ Jun–end Aug Mon–Sat 9–8, Sun 10–6; Sep–end May Mon–Sat 9–5, Sun 10–6 🍴 Many cafés and restaurants 🚇 Federal Triangle 🎟 Free

The Old Post Office

Cartoon depicting jazz musician Duke Ellington, displayed in the National Museum of American History

Along the Mall

This walk along the grassy Mall will take you past DC's most famous landmarks and give you a good look at the soul of the city.

DISTANCE: 3 miles (4.8km) **ALLOW:** 3 hours

START

US CAPITOL (▷ 60–61)
🚻 J6 🚇 Capitol South, Union Station

1 Start on the west steps of the Capitol. Look west toward the Washington Monument (▷ 46–47) across the green expanse of the National Mall, designed more than 200 years ago by Pierre L'Enfant.

2 Descend the stairs, skirt the Reflecting Pool, and walk down the center of the Mall. This area is a center of activity for Washington. In summer Washingtonians play softball here and enjoy a wide range of festivals and the Independence Day Celebration.

3 As you walk down the Mall, you will pass the Smithsonian's greatest hits, along with the National Gallery of Art (▷ 43). Halfway down the Mall on your left you will find an old-fashioned carousel.

4 As the Capitol grows smaller behind you, the Washington Monument has been growing larger. From its base you can see east back down the Mall and west to the Lincoln Memorial (▷ 39). From the top of the obelisk, you can see virtually the entire city.

END

JEFFERSON MEMORIAL (▷ 37)
🚻 F8 🚇 Smithsonian is a 15-minute walk

8 Less than a quarter mile down you will find the FDR Memorial (▷ 37). And, if you follow the path along the Tidal Basin another quarter mile you will see the Jefferson Memorial (▷ 37).

7 Near the Korean War Veterans Memorial (▷ 49), cross Independence Avenue and walk along the road until the sidewalk splits to the right. Follow the right fork around the Tidal Basin.

6 Say hello to Abe, and then go and check out the Vietnam and Korean War memorials (▷ 48, 49) to the northeast and southeast.

5 Walk west toward the Lincoln Memorial. Along the way you will pass the National World War II Memorial (▷ 50), the newest addition to the mall, and the Reflecting Pool, where crowds stood to listen to Martin Luther King Jr. speak in 1963.

THE MALL

WALK

Shopping

MUSEUM OF NATURAL HISTORY (▷ 50)
Three separate gift shops at this museum stock items ranging from dinosaur skeleton model kits to well-made jewelry and geodes.
➕ G6 ✉ Constitution Avenue and 10th Street NW
☎ 202/633–1000
🕐 Daily 10–5.30
🚇 Smithsonian, Federal Triangle

NATIONAL AIR AND SPACE MUSEUM (▷ 40–41)
A three-floor temple to aviation and its knickknacks, this gift shop stocks "astronaut" food, toy rockets, model planes and kites.
➕ H7 ✉ Independence Avenue and 4th Street SW
☎ 202/633–1000
🕐 Daily 10–5.30 🚇 L'Enfant Plaza

NATIONAL GALLERY OF ART (▷ 43)
On the ground floor of the West Building, this gallery shop carries high-quality prints, art stationery, scarves, ties and jewelry, along with other items dependent on the current traveling exhibition in the galleries

housed above. Also gallery guides and catalogs.
➕ H6 ✉ 6th Street and Constitution Avenue NW
☎ 202/842–6941
🕐 Mon–Sat 10–5, Sun 11–6
🚇 Archives–Navy Memorial

NATIONAL MUSEUM OF THE AMERICAN INDIAN (▷ 44)
This museum's two gift shops feature high-grade textiles, jewelry, crafts and games made by Native American artisans.
➕ H7 ✉ 4th Street SW and Independence Avenue
☎ 202/633–1000
🕐 Daily 10–5.30
🚇 Federal Center SW

Restaurants

PRICES
Prices are approximate, based on a 3-course meal for one person.
$$$	over $50
$$	$30–$50
$	under $30

CITYZEN ($$$)
Served in the Mandarin Oriental hotel (▷ 112), top chef Eric Ziebold's creative modern American dishes delight the palette with prime ingredients.
➕ H7 ✉ 1330 Maryland Avenue SW ☎ 202/787–6868
🕐 Tue–Sat dinner
🚇 Smithsonian, 10-min walk

MITSITAM CAFÉ ($$)
In the National Museum of the American Indian, this café offers a sampling of Native American

SEAFOOD SOUTHWEST
For a lively and colorful scene, head to the Southwest Fish Wharf (➕ G6 ✉ 1100 Maine Avenue SW), a floating seafood market at the Potomac River waterfront. From barges and boats, vendors hawk live blue crabs and a wide variety of fish; shucked shellfish, spiced shrimp and fried fish are available.

cuisines from across the Americas, including cedar-planked juniper salmon and buffalo chili on fry bread.
➕ H7 ✉ 4th Street and Independence Avenue SW
☎ 202/633–1000 🕐 Daily 10–5 🚇 Federal Center SW

PAVILION CAFÉ ($)
www.pavilioncafe.com
With a view of the Sculpture Garden (▷ 49), Pavilion serves up a tasty collection of paninis, wraps and salads.
➕ H6 ✉ 700 Constitution Avenue ☎ 202/289–3360
🕐 Daily lunch, dinner
🚇 Archives–Navy Memorial

Dominated by federal buildings, Capitol Hill is home to the Capitol building, Union Station, the Supreme Court and the Library of Congress. Neighborhoods of Victorian rowhouses stretch from these buildings east.

5

G Place

**National
Postal
Museum**

G Street

G Street

**Union
Station**

G

NEW JERSEY AVENUE

F Street

Union
Station

NORTH CAPITOL STREET

COLUMBUS CIRCLE

MASSACHUSETTS

E Street

Street

Street

2nd Street

6

C St

1st

LOUISIANA AVENUE

JERSEY AVENUE

D

Union
Station
Plaza

Delaware Avenue

Street

C

2nd Street

Street

PENNSYLVANIA AVENUE

**Department
of Labor**

CONSTITUTION

AVENUE

3RD STREET

Maryland Avenue

**Grant
Memorial**

US Capitol

**Visitor
Center**

**US Supreme
Court**

2ND STREET

**Folger Shakespeare
Library & Theater**

1ST STREET

**US Botanic
Garden**

**Library
of
Congress**

**Adams
Building**

7

INDEPENDENCE AVENUE

C Street

2nd Street

1st

WASHINGTON AVENUE

1st Street

C Street

NEW JERSEY AVENUE

SOUTH CAPITOL STREET

D

**Madison
Building**

Street

Street

**Capitol
South**

1st Street

2nd

Street

Ivy St

North

E

Street

**Duddington
Place**

E

F Street

8

0 ————— 250 m

0 ————— 250 yds

H   **J**   **K**

Library of Congress

Library interior (opposite); the Torch of Learning atop the dome (left); Library of Congress (right)

Even in a city chockablock with archives and libraries, the Library of Congress is the mother lode. One of the world's largest libraries and the de facto national library contains more than 128 million items, in 460 languages, on 530 miles (853km) of shelves.

A universal approach Congress appropriated funds for a library in 1800. Unfortunately, it was destroyed by the British when they sacked the Capitol in 1814. Thomas Jefferson's personal library, one of the finest in the world, then became the nucleus of the new collection. Jefferson's universal approach to knowledge and book collection became the philosophy for the Library itself, despite its intended purpose to be a resource for congresspeople and their staffs. The Library now files more than 10,000 new books a day, all copyrighted in the US. The Library has also collected random historical items including the contents of Lincoln's pockets on the evening he was shot, original scores by Beethoven and Brahms, and props belonging to Houdini.

Room to read The Italian Renaissance Jefferson Building houses the Library's Main Reading Room, a mecca for scholars. A dozen figures representing the countries or empires that were pivotal in the creation of Western Civilization look down from the apex of the 160ft (48.8m) dome. It is supported by columns topped by female figures representing the aspects of civilized life and thought, including religion, commerce, history and art.

THE BASICS

www.loc.gov

K7

1st Street and Independence Avenue SE

202/707–8000

Mon–Sat 8.30–4.30

Free

Excellent. Visitor Services 202/707–9779 provides American Sign Language interpretation

Cafeteria, coffee shop, Montpelier Restaurant

Capitol South

Tours begin at the Jefferson Building Mon–Sat 10.30, 11.30, 1.30, 2.30, 3.30 (Sat no 3.30 tour). Library resources are open to over-18s pursuing research

HIGHLIGHTS

● Torch of Learning on green copper dome
● Beaux Arts design
● Main Reading Room
● Sculpture inside and out
● View of the Capitol from the Madison Building cafeteria

US Botanic Garden

A microcosm of the many climates and environments represented in the US, the Botanic Garden lets you experience the desert of Arizona even when it's cold out, and blooms flower all year. December's poinsettia display is a crowd pleaser.

Exotic glasshouse In 1838, Congress authorized Lieutenant Charles Wilkes, a surly captain said to be the inspiration for Melville's Captain Ahab, and his crew to circle the globe so that they might provide more accurate charts for the whaling industry. Wilkes returned in 1842 with a collection of exotic plant species, and Congress rekindled dormant plans for a botanical garden. The present 40,000sq ft (3,716sq m) conservatory, an attractive combination of iron-and-glass greenhouse and stone orangeries, was erected in 1931. Following a

A tall cactus in the massive glasshouse at the US Botanic Garden (left); a tranquil escape from the crowds on the Mall: the Conservatory housing lush tropical plants and trees (right)

four-year, $33.5 million renovation, the Garden is now home to more than 4,000 plants.

Flowers for all seasons The main entrance hall serves as a seasonal gallery displaying by turns Christmas poinsettias, tulips and hyacinths, or chrysanthemums. The Conservatory's 12 viewing areas feature plants grown for different uses and in different environments—from high desert flora to the jungle and from coffee and chocolate trees to plants that help us fight cancer. Tucked in the gardens are four specimens—the Vessel Fern, the Ferocious Blue Cycad and two Sago Palms—that are believed to be directly related to those brought back on the Wilkes expedition. The fountain in an adjacent park was sculpted by Frederic Bartholdi (1834–1904), designer of the Statue of Liberty. The park also highlights home landscaping.

THE BASICS

www.usbg.gov
➕ J7
✉ 1st Street SW and Independence Avenue (100 Maryland Avenue NE)
☎ 202/225–8333
🕐 Conservatory daily 10–5. Bartholdi Park dawn to dusk
✋ Free
♿ Excellent
🚇 Federal Center SW

US Capitol

HIGHLIGHTS

● Rotunda
● Frescos by Constantino Brumidi
● Paintings by John Trumbull
● Visit to the House or Senate Chambers

TIP

● Check in advance to see when Congress is in session, and plan accordingly. Try to arrange a tour through a congressperson's office; the Senate Office Buildings and the Capitol subway are certainly worth seeing.

Imitated on state buildings throughout the country, the Capitol dome makes an iconic backdrop for television newscasters and politicians as a symbol of American democracy. A state-of-the-art underground visitor center tells you more.

Icon The 4,500-ton, cast-iron dome was an engineering feat when undertaken in 1851 by Capitol architect Charles Walter and US Army Quarter-master General Montgomery Meigs. It became a political symbol before it was even half finished: The Civil War broke out while it was under construction, and the Capitol housed the wounded. Many advised President Lincoln to halt work on the building, but he was adamant that progress continue as "a sign we intend the Union shall go on." The dome was completed in 1863.

Clockwise from far left: The famous dome of the US Capitol; visitors inspecting the Rotunda; the Capitol is visible from nearly every part of the city, as it stands at the very heart of Washington; the columns of the Capitol; classical figures adorning the Capitol's exterior

Founding Fathers Visitors to the Capitol can tour the old Supreme Court Chamber where famous cases have been decided; Statuary Hall, where the House of Representatives first met; the old Senate Chamber, where Webster, Clay and Calhoun famously sparred; and the wonderfully ornate Brumidi Corridors. But arguably the crowning moment of a Capitol tour is viewing the Rotunda, located under the Capitol dome. Eight gigantic murals, four by George Washington's aide John Trumbull, depict scenes from the colonies and the revolutionary period. The Apotheosis of Washington, visible through the eye of the inner dome, depicts classical deities surrounding the first president. Constantino Brumidi (1805–80), who painted the fresco, was said to consort with "ladies of the night," whose likenesses then appeared as ample maidens ministering to George Washington.

THE BASICS

www.visitthecapitol.com

🔹 J6

✉ East Capitol and 1st Street

☎ 202/226–8000

🕐 Daily 8.340–4.30

♿ Free 🔵 Excellent

🍴 Dining Room (by invitation), cafeterias

Ⓜ Capitol South, Union Station

❓ Tours run Mon–Sat 8.50–3.20 and are free but require passes. US citizens can ask their elected representatives; anyone can book online. A limited number of same-day passes are available daily at the tour kiosks of the Capitol or the information desks at the Visitor Center

Union Station

The Beaux Arts Union Station (left) and the vaulted ceiling of Union Station's Main Hall (right)

THE BASICS

www.unionstationdc.com
+ K5
✉ 50 Massachusetts Avenue NE
☎ 202/289–1908
🕐 Daily 24 hours for train service; stores and restaurants generally Mon–Sat 10–9, Sun 12–6
♿ Free
♿ Excellent
🍴 Many
Ⓜ Union Station

HIGHLIGHTS

● Main Hall
● Statues of Roman legionnaires
● East Hall
● Presidential Waiting Room
● Columbus Plaza

Union Station is more than just a connection point for Washington's railroads and Metro. This magnificent building brings together shops, restaurants and a cinema, all enjoyed by a teeming mass of office workers running errands, political dealmakers, bureaucrats and tourists.

World's largest Architect Daniel H. Burnham lived up to his motto, "Make No Little Plans," when he undertook the consolidation of DC's train lines early last century. His vaulted, white-marble, Beaux Arts Union Station was the largest train station in the world when it opened in 1908. It is still one of the most visited spots in DC, a destination for up to 30 million people each year. Visitors are greeted by a grand memorial to Christopher Columbus, sculpted by Lorado Taft, which punctuates the park in front of the station. But attention quickly turns to the massive Doric colonnade and the neoclassical sculptures above—depicting fire, electricity, freedom, imagination, agriculture and mechanics.

More than trains Directly inside, you enter a cavernous main hall as wide as the Washington Monument is tall. The 96ft-high (29m) coffered ceiling is embellished with 70lbs (32kg) of gold leaf, guarded by 46 Augustus Saint-Gaudens statues of Roman legionnaires. Renovated and reopened in 1988, the building now houses a huge variety of stores and restaurants and an active train terminal and Metro stop. The market-like East Hall has stalls selling items from around the world. There is a large food court downstairs.

Exterior of the US
Supreme Court (left)
and detail of
Contemplation of
Justice (right)

One justice called this 1935 neoclassical building, designed by Cass Gilbert Jr., "bombastically pretentious...for a quiet group of old boys such as the Supreme Court."

Judgments America's highest court may still be "old boy," despite the arrival of Justice Sonia Sotomayor—only the third woman to serve on the Court in its 220-year history—but it has never been quiet. The 1857 Dred Scott decision, which held that Congress had no authority to limit slavery, contributed to the onset of the Civil War. Rulings on abortion have frequently made the plaza in front of the building a focus of civil disobedience. *Brown v. Board of Education* required the integration of schools and bus travel across the land and *Engel v. Vitale* outlawed school prayer. The Court is not televised and the justices, who are appointed for life, seldom give interviews.

Law in action The steps up to the colonnaded entrance are flanked by two white-marble allegorical figures by James Earle Fraser, depicting *The Contemplation of Justice* and *The Authority of Law*. The magnificent bronze entrance doors, designed by John Donnely Jr., lead into an entrance hall adorned with busts of all the former chief justices. When the Court is in session you can join the "three-minute line" and glimpse proceedings from the Standing Gallery. A statue of John Marshall, Chief Justice from 1755 to 1835, dominates the street level where a short film and changing exhibits describe the work of the Court.

THE BASICS

www.supremecourtus.gov
✚ K6
✉ 1st and East Capitol streets NE
☎ 202/479-3211
🕐 Mon–Fri 9–4.30
🎟 Free
♿ Excellent
🍴 Cafeteria
🚇 Capitol South, Union Station
❓ Lectures on the half-hour when the Court is not in session 9–3.30

HIGHLIGHTS
- Bronze entrance doors
- Plaza sculpture
- Busts of chief justices
- Film and exhibits on Court history
- The Court in session

More to See

EASTERN MARKET

www.easternmarket.net

Newly renovated after a fire in 2006, this fresh food market has been in continuous operation since 1873. Local artisan wares, too (▷ 66).
➕ L7 ✉ 7th and C streets SE ⏰ Tue–Sat 7–6, Sun 9–4; Flea market: weekends 9–6 🚇 Eastern Market

FOLGER SHAKESPEARE LIBRARY

www.folger.edu

The world's most comprehensive collection of Shakespeare's works is included in this library of 275,000 books, manuscripts and paintings from and about the European Renaissance.
➕ K7 ✉ 201 E Capitol Street SE ☎ 202/544-7077 ⏰ For researchers Mon–Sat 10–5. Guided tours Mon–Fri 11am, 3pm; Sat 11am, 1pm; garden tours Apr–end Oct every 3rd Sat, 10am, 11am 🚇 Capitol South 🎫 Free

FREDERICK DOUGLASS MUSEUM

www.nahc.org/fd

The first Washington home of one of the country's most celebrated abolitionists now houses two rooms of Douglass memorabilia and the Hall of Fame for Caring Americans.
➕ K6 ✉ 320 A Street NE ☎ 202/547-4273 ⏰ By appointment only 🚇 Capitol South, Union Station

GRANT MEMORIAL

Cool and calm Ulysses S. Grant, Civil War general and former president, is honored atop his horse in this memorial, the third largest equestrian statue in the world.
➕ J6 ✉ 1st Street NW at foot of Capitol Hill ⏰ Daily 24 hours 🚇 Federal Center SW 🎫 Free

NATIONAL POSTAL MUSEUM

www.postalmuseum.si.edu

Tributes to the Pony Express, 11 million stamps from around the world and an array of interactive exhibits illuminate the history of the US Postal Service in this family-oriented museum.
➕ J5 ✉ 2 Massachusetts Avenue NE across from Union Station ☎ 202/633-5555 ⏰ Daily 10–5.30 🚇 Union Station 🎫 Free

The Grant Memorial at the foot of Capitol Hill

MORE TO SEE · CAPITOL HILL

Federal Route

Capitol Hill is where you can get closest to the action. Take this walk to catch a glimpse of a Congressional staffer's daily life.

DISTANCE: 1.75 miles (2.8km) **ALLOW:** 2 hours

START

UNION STATION (▷ 62)
✚ K5 🚇 Union Station

❶ Start at the Columbus memorial in front of the stunning Beaux Arts Union Station (▷ 62).

❷ Head toward the US Capitol (▷ 60–61) on Delaware Avenue. On the way you will pass the Russell Senate Office Building, where many Senators' offices and their staff are housed.

❸ If you don't have time to go inside the Capitol, take time to walk around it. Head west after you cross Constitution Avenue and follow the large circular path around the front of the Capitol.

❹ You will pass the Peace Monument before reaching the Grant Memorial (▷ 64) due west of the Capitol. Take the opportunity to climb the stairs for a view down the Mall toward the Washington Monument (▷ 46–47).

END

EASTERN MARKET OR BARRACKS ROW (▷ 64) ✚ L7 🚇 Eastern Market

❽ From here you can enjoy some lively shopping at Eastern Market (▷ 64, 66), north on 7th Street, or stop for food and drinks on the quickly gentrifying Barracks Row, south on 8th Street.

❼ Depending on the time of day, you will see congressional staff grabbing a quick lunch or relaxing after a long day in the bars and restaurants that line the south side of Pennsylvania Avenue. Continue to the Eastern Market Metro stop.

❻ The path ends at 1st Street SE and Independence Avenue. Taking Independence east you will pass the buildings of the Library of Congress (▷ 57) before turning right on Pennsylvania Avenue.

❺ Walk back down the stairs and continue south on the path around the Capitol. You will pass the Garfield Memorial and the US Botanic Garden (▷ 58–59) before heading up the hill, with the House Office Buildings on your right.

Shopping

A LITTERI
www.litteris.com
In the heart of the wholesale market since 1932, this Italian old-timer stocks more than 100 types of olive oils and wines to go with any pasta dish you can dream up.
✚ L4 ✉ 517 Morse Street NE
☎ 202/544-0183
🕐 Tue–Wed 8–4, Thu–Fri 8–5, Sat 8–3 🚇 New York Avenue

ALVEAR STUDIO
This home-furnishings store gathers high-end artisanal products from around the world.
✚ L8 ✉ 705 8th Street SE
☎ 202/546-8434
🕐 Tue–Thu 11–7, Fri 11–8, Sat 10–7, Sun 12–6
🚇 Eastern Market

BACKSTAGE, INC
http://backstagebooks.com
This theater store is packed with dancewear and shoes, costumes, masks and wigs, and stage makeup. It also carries plays and scripts, theater magazines and sheet music.
✚ L8 ✉ 545 8th Street SE
☎ 202/544-5744
🕐 Mon–Sat 11–7
🚇 Eastern Market

CAPITOL HILL BOOKS
It's near impossible for this store to stock any more used books. Don't yodel too loud, you might find yourself crushed under an avalanche of foreign language books in the bathroom. Seriously.
✚ L7 ✉ 657 C Street SE
☎ 202/544-1621
🕐 Mon–Fri 11.30–6, Sat–Sun 9–6 🚇 Eastern Market

DAWN PRICE BABY
Toys and clothes for tots are the specialty at this welcoming boutique.
✚ L7 ✉ 325 7th Street SE
☎ 202/543-2920
🕐 Tue–Fri 11–6, Sat–Sun 10–5 🚇 Eastern Market

EASTERN MARKET
Here you'll find fresh produce under the canopy on weekends and fresh meats, fish, cheeses, baked goods and prepared foods (especially Mexican and Italian) six days a week. Saturday also brings a craft market, with a high volume of handmade jewelry, and Sunday a flea market.
✚ L7 ✉ C and 7th streets SE
🕐 Tue–Sat 7–6, Sun 9–4; flea market Sat–Sun 9–6
🚇 Eastern Market

MARKET MENU

For fresh produce and arti-sanal meats, check out Eastern Market (7th Street SE and North Carolina Avenue. Tue–Sat 7–6, Sun 9–4), Dupont Circle Market (Q Street NW and Massachusetts Avenue. Jan–end Mar 10am–1pm, Mar–end Dec 9am–1pm), or the Adams-Morgan Farmers Market (18th Street NW and Columbia Road. May–end Dec Sat 8–1).

FAIRY GODMOTHER
This store caters to kids of all ages, who will find a multicultural smorgas-bord of books and toys.
✚ L7 ✉ 319 7th Street SE
☎ 202/544-5474
🕐 Mon–Fri 10.30–6, Sat 10–5
🚇 Eastern Market

FORECAST
Well known for their excellent service and for their stylish, classic cloth-ing for women, Forecast also stocks homewares and accessories.
✚ L7 ✉ 218 7th Street SE
☎ 202/547-7337
🕐 Tue–Fri 11–7, Sat 10–6, Sun 12–5 🚇 Eastern Market

UNION STATION
The city's main railway station also doubles as one of America's most pleasant shopping malls where you can wander along marble-floored avenues under vaulted ceilings. Good for gifts.
✚ K5 ✉ 50 Massachusetts Avenue NE ☎ 202/289-1908
🕐 Mon–Sat 10–9, Sun 12–6
🚇 Union Station

THE VILLAGE GALLERY
Flax is a "favorite" at this friendly home and garden full to the brim with women's clothing and accessories.
✚ L7 ✉ 705 North Carolina Avenue SE ☎ 202/546-3040
🕐 Tue–Fri 11–6, Sat 10–6, Sun 12–4 🚇 Eastern Market

Entertainment and Nightlife

CAPITOL LOUNGE
Popular among thirsty Hill staffers at happy hour, "Cap Lounge" also caters to those hoping to catch the latest soccer match.
➕ K7 ✉ 231 Pennsylvania Avenue SE ☎ 202/547-2098 🕐 Mon 4pm–2am, Tue–Thu 11am–2am, Fri 11am–3am, Sat 10am–3am, Sun 10am–2am 🚇 Capitol South

COOLIDGE AUDITORIUM
www.loc.gov
With near-perfect acoustics and sightlines, this Library of Congress auditorium draws talented musicians from all genres.
➕ K7 ✉ 1st Street and Independence Avenue SE ☎ 202/707-5502 🚇 Capitol South

THE DUBLINER
www.dublinerdc.com
This Irish pub, a favorite with Senate staff, often features live music.

➕ J5 ✉ 4 F Street NW ☎ 202/737-3773 🕐 Sun–Thu 11am–2am, Fri– Sat 11am–3am 🚇 Union Station

FOLGER SHAKESPEARE THEATRE
www.folger.edu
Daring and sharp productions of the Bard's work are staged here in this re-creation of an Elizabethan theater.
➕ K7 ✉ 201 East Capitol Street SE ☎ 202/544-7077 🚇 Union Station

HAWK'N'DOVE
This dark-wood-panel bar is frequented by lobbyists, politicos and interns.
➕ K7 ✉ 329 Pennsylvania Avenue SE ☎ 202/543-3300 🕐 Sun–Thu 10am–2am, Fri–Sat 10am–3am 🚇 Capitol South

LOCKHEED MARTIN IMAX THEATER
www..si.edu/imax
The giant IMAX screeen at the Smithsonian Air and Space Museum (▷ 40–41) shows larger than life nature, wildlife and space films.
➕ H7 ✉ Independence Avenue at 4th Street SW ☎ 202/633-4629, 866/ 868-7444 🕐 Check for times 🚇 L'Enfant Plaza, Smithsonian

SONOMA WINE BAR
A soothing bar with exposed brick walls and hardwood floors, Sonoma offers a large selection of wine by the glass and a

knowledgeable staff.
➕ K7 ✉ 223 Pennsylvania Avenue SE ☎ 202/544-8088 🕐 Mon–Fri 11.30–2,30, 5.30–10.30, Sat 5.30–11, Sun 5.30–9 🚇 Capitol South

TOP OF THE HILL
A wood-paneled martini lounge popular among congressional staff, Top of the Hill sits atop the more casual Politiki.
➕ K7 ✉ 319 Pennsylvania Avenue SE ☎ 202/546-7782 🕐 Mon–Thu 5.30pm–2am, Fri 5.30pm–3am, Sat 7pm– 3am, Fri–Sat 10am–3pm 🚇 Capitol South

TORTILLA COAST
Solid Tex-Mex and well-priced margaritas pull droves of young Hill staffers to this watering hole right after work.
➕ K7 ✉ 400 1st Street SE ☎ 202/546-6768 🕐 Mon–Wed 11.30–10, Thu–Fri 11.30–11, Sat 11.30–10, Sun 11–9 🚇 Capitol South

SPECTATOR SPORTS

If you are here in fall (autumn), you will hear about the Redskins American football team, but season-ticket holders have all the seats. You'll have better luck seeing the Wizards play basketball or the Capitals play hockey, both at the Verizon Center in downtown Washington. Look on line for single ticket sales or try www.stubhub.com/washington -redskins-tickets

MOVIES

Check the daily newspapers for mainstream first-run movies–theaters are scattered throughout the city. For "arthouse" and foreign films, try the **Landmark's Bethesda Row Cinema** (☎ 301/652–7273) or **Landmark's E Street Cinema** (☎ 202/452–7672) The **Library of Congress** (☎ 202/707– 5677) often shows old movies, including some silent films.

Restaurants

BANANA CAFÉ AND PIANO BAR ($)

www.bananacafedc.com
Stick with the Cuban and Puerto Rican dishes at this lively, colorful eatery that features live entertainment each night.

➕ L8 ✉ 500 8th Street SE ☎ 202/543-5906 🕐 Mon–Sat lunch, dinner; Sun brunch, dinner 🚇 Eastern Market

BELGA CAFÉ ($–$$)

www.belgacafe.com
This smart Belgian restaurant is best at brunch with its unique, but subtly flavored, options, including goat cheese waffles with red pepper coulis and poached eggs with salmon and asparagus.

➕ L8 ✉ 514 8th Street SE ☎ 202/544-0100 🕐 Daily lunch, dinner; Sat–Sun brunch 🚇 Eastern Market

BISTRO BIS ($$–$$$)

www.bistrobis.com
In the Hotel George, Bis offers an extensive wine list to complement its solid French menu. The warm and elegant environment draws power players, celebrities and Senators.

➕ J6 ✉ 15 E Street NW ☎ 202/661-2700 🕐 Daily breakfast, lunch and dinner 🚇 Union Station

CHARLIE PALMER STEAK ($$$)

www.charliepalmer.com/steak_dc
This sleek restaurant with a view of the Capitol is known for its high-power clientele and quality steaks masterfully prepared by chef Bryan Voltaggi. The experience is rounded out by a deep American wine list.

➕ J6 ✉ 101 Constitution Avenue NW ☎ 202/547-8100 🕐 Lunch Mon–Fri, dinner daily 🚇 Union Station

FIREHOOK ($)

www.firehook.com
This popular bakery churns out tasty sandwiches on fresh-baked bread, along with an array of fresh salads.

➕ K7 ✉ 215 Pennsylvania Avenue SE ☎ 202/544-7003

UNION STATION

Alongside the train services, shopping opportunities and world-class exhibitions you'll find a huge variety of eating places at Union Station (▷ 68). Formal restaurants serve American, Japanese, Mexican, Korean, Filipino, Chinese and Indian cuisine, and there are plenty of places to stop for a quick cup of coffee, a tasty light lunch or a fast-food option.

🕐 Mon–Fri 6.30am–7pm, Sat–Sun 7–5 🚇 Capitol South

LA LOMA ($–$$)

The Mexican cuisine may not be too hot, but the gossip-filled whisperings of congressional staff lubricated by margaritas is enough to satisfy.

➕ K6 ✉ 316 Massachusetts Avenue NE ☎ 202/548-2550 🕐 Daily lunch, dinner 🚇 Union Station

MARKET LUNCH ($)

This counter-service eatery features crab cakes, fried fish and North Carolina barbecue.

➕ L6 ✉ 225 7th Street SE ☎ 202/547-8444 🕐 Wed–Sun breakfast, lunch 🚇 Eastern Market

MONTMARTRE ($$)

A traditional but exceptional French bistro with an open kitchen and friendly environment. Braised rabbit leg over pasta is a favorite.

➕ L6 ✉ 327 7th Street SE ☎ 202/544-1244 🕐 Daily lunch, dinner 🚇 Eastern Market

TAQUERIA NACIONALE ($)

Owned by James Beard award-winning chef, Ann Cashion, this taqueria serves up stripped-down, gourmet lunch and breakfast to go.

➕ J6 ✉ 400 N Capitol Street NW ☎ 202/737-7070 🕐 Daily breakfast, lunch 🚇 Union Station

DC's wealthiest neighborhood first became popular in the 1960s and has grown more affluent ever since. A perfect spot for outdoor shopping, Georgetown brings droves in the warmer months.

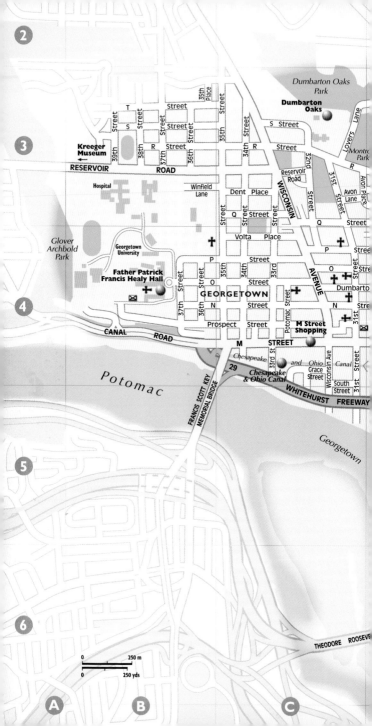

Oak Hill
Cemetery

treet

DUMBARTON
BRIDGE

Q   Street

P

Waterside   Drive

PARKWAY

POTOMAC

Rock Creek

26th St

30th
Street

29th

28th

27th

Olive   Street

Street

25th   Street

24th   Street

N

23RD

22nd

Street

M   STREET

PENNSYLVANIA

L
Street

K   STREET

NEW

HAMPSHIRE

Washington
Circle

AVENUE

21st

Street

P   Street

O   Street

Newport
Place

Street

Street

Street

Street

Street

Foggy
Bottom - GWU

AND

Watergate
Complex

John F Kennedy
Center

Channel

CREEK

66

P

P

VIRGINIA

ROCK

MEMORIAL   BRIDGE

AVENUE

23RD

State
Department

George Washington
University

21st

Street

I

H

G

F   Street

Street

Street

24th   Street

22nd

Street

Street

21st

D

E

Georgetown Shopping

Jackie Kennedy first drew the rich and powerful to Georgetown with the cocktail parties she held during her husband's time in the US Senate. They stayed, populating the Federalist town houses that line this neighborhood's narrow tree-lined streets. Inevitably, Georgetown quickly became, and has remained, DC's upscale shopping destination.

Wisconsin and M Metro inaccessibility does not deter crowds from Georgetown's main intersection, full of chic shops that stretch north on Wisconsin Avenue and east on M Street. Warm months are particularly busy as tourists and locals flock to the shops they know—Banana Republic, Urban Outfitters and Coach, among countless others. An indoor mall on the southwest corner of the intersection, the Shops at Georgetown with J. Crew, Ann Taylor, Anthropologie and H&M, is equally popular.

Not just an outdoor mall Those with more fastidious tastes or specific needs will also find boutiques, antiques shops, home furnishings and bookstores. Dubbed "Georgetown's Design District," Cady's Alley, off 33rd Street just south of M Street, is lined with mid- to high-end home furnishing galleries. Georgetown's fine antiques shops can be found mainly on the eastern section of M Street before it crosses Rock Creek Parkway. Some of the better independent shops huddle farther up Wisconsin Avenue on Book Hill, just south of the Georgetown Library.

THE BASICS

➕ C4

✉ Mainly M Street NW between 30th Street and 34th Street and Wisconsin Avenue NW between South Street and R Street

♿ Limited

HIGHLIGHTS

● The Shops at Georgetown
● A stroll along the C&O Canal towpath
● The view from the Georgetown Library
● Wandering among the Federalist mansions to the northeast of the intersection between Wisconsin Avenue and M Street

John F. Kennedy Center

Bust of Kennedy inside the Kennedy Center (left) and the Hall of Nations (right)

With six theaters, this national cultural center covers 8 acres (3.2ha) and is the jewel of the city's arts scene. The roof terrace provides a stunning 360-degree view of Washington and the Potomac.

The seat of the arts   Opened in 1971, Edward Durrell Stone's white-marble box overlooks the Potomac River next to the Watergate complex. In 1958, when President Eisenhower (1890–1969) signed the National Cultural Center Act, it was the first time that the US government financed a structure dedicated to the performing arts. As a living memorial to President Kennedy, and subsequently a beneficiary of federal funding, the center is still a unique public-private partnership. When the Kennedy Center opened, the Washington performing arts scene joined the major leagues. It now hosts more than 3,000 performances a year by some of the world's most talented artists.

Hall of States   The red carpet in the Hall of States and the parallel Hall of Nations leads to the Grand Foyer, where visitors are greeted by a 3,000lb (1,363kg) bronze bust of President Kennedy. This 630ft-long (192m) hall blazes from the light of 18 Orrefors crystal chandeliers, donated by Sweden and reflected in 60ft-high (18.3m) mirrors, a gift from Belgium. One end of the hall is devoted to the Millennium Stage, where free performances are given every evening. The building also contains an opera house, a concert hall, two stage theaters, a jazz club, a movie theater, a theater lab and the Performing Arts Library of the Library of Congress.

More to See

CHESAPEAKE & OHIO CANAL

www.nps.gov/choh

Built in 1825, this tree-lined canal runs parallel to the Potomac River from Georgetown to Cumberland, Maryland. Mule-drawn canal boats are operated by the National Park Service. The wide towpath is a great place to stroll or ride a bike.

➕ C4 ✉ C&O Canal Visitor Center: 1057 Thomas Jefferson Street NW ☎ Canal boat rides 202/653–5190 (Wed, Sun 11, 1.30, 3) 🕐 Visitor Center: Wed–Sun 9–4.30 🚇 M Street: 30, 32, 34, 35, 36 ✋ Free. Canal boat tour moderate; under 3 free

DUMBARTON OAKS

www.doaks.org

In 1944, the international conference leading to the formation of the United Nations was held at this estate, also known for its formal garden, replete with an orangery, rose garden, wisteria and magnificent shaded terraces. This a must for anyone interested in gardens or who just wants to rest for a few moments surrounded by blazing nature.

➕ C3 ✉ 31st and R streets NW ☎ 202/ 339–6400 🕐 Nov–14 Mar Tue–Sun 2–5, 15 Mar–end Oct 2–6 🚇 Dupont Circle, then bus D2 ✋ Garden moderate; museum free

FATHER PATRICK FRANCIS HEALY HALL, GEORGETOWN UNIVERSITY

www.georgetown.edu

This 1879 baronial fantasy honors the first black Catholic priest and bishop in America, who later became president of Georgetown University.

➕ B4 ✉ 37th and O streets NW ☎ 202/687–5055 🕐 Daily 24 hours 🚇 Rosslyn, then bus 38B ✋ Free

KREEGER MUSEUM

www.kreegermuseum.org

Built by David and Carmen Kreeger to be both museum and home, this Philip Johnson mansion now solely houses art, mainly the work of the male masters of the last two centuries.

➕ Off map at A2 ✉ 2401 Foxhall Road NW ☎ 877/337–3050 🕐 Tue–Fri tours 10.30, 1.30 (reservations required), Sat 10–4 (no reservations required) 🚇 Tenley Town, then taxi or walk ✋ Moderate

Towpath of the Chesapeake & Ohio Canal

Healy Building, Georgetown University

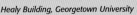

GEORGETOWN/FOGGY BOTTOM

★

MORE TO SEE

Waterfront Walk

See one of Washington's oldest and most stately neighborhoods from a variety of angles and perspectives.

DISTANCE: 1.5 miles (2.4km) **ALLOW:** 2 hours

START

JOHN F. KENNEDY CENTER (▷ 74)
✚ D6 🚇 Foggy Bottom

END

GEORGETOWN UNIVERSITY (▷ 75)
✚ B4 🚇 Rosslyn (a 20-minute walk)

1 Start with a view of the Georgetown waterfront from the terrace of the Kennedy Center (▷ 74).

2 Exit through the front of the building; take a left and then another left onto F Street. Cross the parkway that runs under the Kennedy Center Terrace and turn right on the path by the Potomac.

3 Follow the Potomac north and catch a glimpse of the infamous Watergate Hotel on your right. The path curves behind the boathouse and then back to the river.

4 Stroll on the boardwalk past the restaurants and bars along the Georgetown waterfront. Then take a right on the edge of the park and cross onto 31st Street. The movie theater on your left used to be the Georgetown incinerator.

8 Heading left on Volta Street will take you to the Georgetown University Campus. The Georgetown Library is 0.25 miles (0.4km) farther up Wisconsin Avenue. From the small park behind the Library you get a great view over Georgetown.

7 Turn right on Wisconsin Avenue and follow it up the hill. Washington DC's most expensive houses sit on the tree-lined streets to your right.

6 Take a left on M Street. You are now entering the shopping district (▷ 73), the epicenter of which is at Wisconsin Avenue and M Street.

5 Continue up the hill on 31st Street, crossing over the C&O Canal (▷ 75). You will see Georgetown's old mills to the west. That smokestack was once part of a paper mill.

Shopping

A MANO
"By hand" stocks fine home furnishings crafted by skillful European artisans.
🔲 C3 ✉ 1677 Wisconsin Avenue NW ☎ 202/298–7200 🕐 Mon–Sat 10–6, Sun 12–5

ANTHROPOLOGIE
A mecca of shabby chic carrying homewares, clothing and accessories.
🔲 C4 ✉ 3222 M Street NW ☎ 202/337–1363 🕐 Mon–Sat 10–9, Sun 12–7

BRIDGE STREET BOOKS
This charming rowhouse contains a nice collection of books.
🔲 D4 ✉ 2814 Pennsylvania Avenue NW ☎ 202/965–5200 🕐 Mon–Sat 11–9, Sun 12–6

DESIGN WITHIN REACH
Modern home furnishings from well-known designers set in gallery displays.
🔲 C4 ✉ 3307 Cady's Alley, 3318 M Street NW ☎ 202/339–9480 🕐 Mon–Sat 10–6, Sun 12–6

GEORGETOWN ANTIQUES CENTER
Inside this Victorian town house is the Cherub Gallery, which specializes in art nouveau, art deco and Vienna Secession design periods, and Michael Getz antiques.
🔲 D4 ✉ 2918 M Street NW ☎ Cherub Gallery 202/337–2224; Michael Getz 202/338–3811, 🕐 Mon–Fri 11–5.30, Sat 12–5

HU'S SHOES
On the absolute front edge of fashion, Hu's carries shoes you can't find outside of New York, Paris or Milan.
🔲 D4 ✉ 3005 M Street NW (also at 2906 M Street) ☎ 202/342–0202/342–2020 🕐 Mon–Sat 10–7, Sun 12–5

INTERMIX
Intermix offers hand-picked styles from the "it" list of designers, including the UK's popular Stella McCartney.
🔲 C4 ✉ 3222 M Street NW ☎ 202/298–8080 🕐 Mon–Sat 10–9, Sun 12–6

JEAN PIERRE ANTIQUES
There's no need to go to France: Enjoy this quintessential Georgetown shop that supplies antique furniture to well-heeled locals and famous visitors.
🔲 D4 ✉ 2601 P Street NW ☎ 202/337–1731 🕐 Daily 11–5

BOOKS FOR NIGHT OWLS
You can find bookstores open well into the night in nearly every area of Washington, many with cafés, knowledgeable staff and discounts. In Dupont Circle, is Kramerbooks and Afterwords Café (▷ 90) on 1517 Connecticut Avenue NW, where the store remains open all night on weekends and so does the kitchen.

KIEHL'S
Kiehl's has had a growing following for its skin-care products since 1851.
🔲 D4 ✉ 2601 P Street NW ☎ 202/333–5102 🕐 Mon–Fri 10–9, Sat 10–8, Sun 11–6.30

THE OLD PRINT GALLERY
One of the oldest print and map shops in the US, this gallery stocks antique prints as old as America itself, as well as an impressive collection of *New Yorker* covers.
🔲 C4 ✉ 1220 31st Street NW ☎ 202/965–1818 🕐 Mon–Sat 10–5.30

PAPER SOURCE
This two-floor paper store stocks cute cards, fine stationery and book-binding kits.
🔲 D4 ✉ 3019 M Street NW ☎ 202/298–5545 🕐 Mon–Sat 10–9, Sun 11–7

PUMA
As one of the clothier's "concept" stores, this branch test drives new ideas in a building that exudes cool.
🔲 C4 ✉ 1237 Wisconsin Avenue NW ☎ 202/944–9870 🕐 Mon–Sat 10–8, Sun 11–6

URBAN CHIC
Urban Chic features wearable trends and classics from designers that include Diane von Furstenberg and Catherine Malandrino.
🔲 C3 ✉ 1626 Wisconsin Avenue NW ☎ 202/338–5398 🕐 Mon–Sat 10–7, Sun 12–5

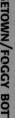

Entertainment and Nightlife

51ST STATE

A straight-up pub decorated in vintage Guinness ads, 51st State draws regulars with its back patio, TVs tuned to sports and chilled drafts.

D4 ✉ 2512 L Street NW ☎ 202/625-2444 ◐ Daily 4pm–2am 🚇 Foggy Bottom

BIRRERIA PARADISO

Downstairs from Pizzeria Paradiso (▷ 80), this temple of beer offers 16 of the world's finest varieties on tap and 80 in bottles.

C4 ✉ 3282 M Street NW ☎ 202/337-1245 ◐ Mon–Thu 11.30–11, Fri–Sat 11.30am–midnight, Sun 12–10

BLUES ALLEY

www.bluesalley.com

A legendary jazz club, made famous in recordings by Dizzy Gillespie, Charlie Byrd and the like, Blues Alley now pulls top national acts.

C4 ✉ Rear 1073 Wisconsin Avenue NW ☎ 202/337-4141 ◐ Daily 6pm–12.30am 🚇 Farragut West, then bus 32 or 38B 💲 Cover charge and minimum charge

CLYDE'S

Truly a "Georgetown'" bar, Clyde's is decked out in dark-wood paneling, and has genuine bartenders and a solid menu.

C4 ✉ 3236 M Street NW ☎ 202/333-9180 ◐ Mon–Thu 11am–midnight, Fri–11am–1am, Sat 10am–1am, Sun 9–midnight

DEGREES

In the heart of what was once Georgetown's incinerator, this elegant watering hole draws well-dressed patrons with its industrial motif.

C4 ✉ Ritz-Carlton Hotel, 3100 South Street NW ☎ 202/912-4100 ◐ Sun–Thu 2.30–11, Fri–Sat 2.30–1

THE GUARDS

This historic Georgetown landmark restaurant, bar, and late night lounge features a glass ceiling with colored lights illuminating a dance floor.

D4 ✉ 2915 M Street NW (cross street 29th Street) ☎ 202/965-2350 ◐ Mon–Thu 11.30am–2am, Fri–Sat 11.30am–3am, Sun 11.30am–2am

JOHN F. KENNEDY CENTER

DC's top spot for renowned performers (▷ 74).

MATÉ

This chic sister to Chi Cha Lounge offers both sushi

HALF-PRICE TICKETS

TICKETplace (406 7th Street NW; 202/842-5387; www.ticketplace.org) offers same-day half-price tickets to a wide variety of shows around town. Sunday and Monday tickets are sold on Monday. There is a 12 percent to 17 percent service charge. Many theaters around town also sell discounted preview week or last-minute tickets.

and ceviche to steal against the saketinis.

C5 ✉ 3101 K Street NW ☎ 202/333-2006 ◐ Sun–Thu 5pm–12.30am, Fri–Sat 5pm–1.30am

MODERN

Comfortable and familiar, Modern plays songs you know—from Outkast to Madonna—in its white-accented, modern space.

C4 ✉ 3287 M Street NW ☎ 202/338-7027 ◐ Tue–Thu 9pm–2am, Fri–Sat 9pm–3am

SEQUOIA

On the Georgetown waterfront with a lovely view over the Potomac.

D5 ✉ 3000 K Street NW ☎ 202/944-4200 ◐ Sun–Tue 11–9, Wed–Thu 11.30–10, Fri–Sat 11.30–11

THOMPSON'S BOAT CENTER

Canoes, rowboats, rowing shells, sailboards and bicycles for rent.

D5 ✉ 2900 Virginia Avenue NW ☎ 202/333-9543 ◐ Rentals: daily 8–5; closed mid-Nov to early Mar 🚇 Foggy Bottom

THE TOMBS

This subterranean bar, adorned with vintage crew prints and oars, is popular among Georgetown students and professors.

B4 ✉ 1226 36th Street NW ☎ 202/337-6668 ◐ Mon–Thu 11.30am–1.15am, Fri 11.30am–2.15am, Sat 11am–2.15am, Sun 9.30am–1.15am

Ristorante Piccolo

Restavrants

PRICES

Prices are approximate, based on a 3-course meal for one person.
$$$ over $50
$$ $30–$50
$ under $30

1789 ($$$)

www.1789restaurant.com
In an historic town house with a large fireplace, 1789 specializes in innovatively prepared game and seafood.
🚇 B4 ✉ 1226 36th Street NW ☎ 202/965-1789 🕐 Mon–Thu 6–10, Fri–Sat 5.30–11, Sun 5.30–10 🚌 Foggy Bottom, then bus 32 or 38B

CAFÉ BONAPARTE ($–$$)

www.cafebonaparte.com
The draw at this charming bistro with dark red walls and a silver ceiling is the delicious sweet and savory crepes. It bills itself as "the quintessential European café, creperie, coffeeshop and bar."
🚇 C4 ✉ 1522 Wisconsin Avenue NW ☎ 202/333-8830 🕐 Mon–Thu 10am–11pm, Fri–Sat 10am–1am, Sun 9am–10pm

DEAN AND DELUCA ($)

www.deandeluca.com
A picnicker's paradise, this grocer carries, among other things, the finest fruit, chocolate and cheese and a dazzling array of gourmet prepared foods.
🚇 C4 ✉ 3276 M Street NW ☎ 202/342-2500 🕐 Daily 8–8 store; 9–8 café

FIVE GUYS ($)

www.fiveguys.com
Another branch of this popular hangout (▷ 31).
🚇 C4 ✉ 1335 Wisconsin Avenue ☎ 202/337-0400 🕐 Sun–Thu 11–11, Fri–Sat 11am–4am

LEOPOLD'S KAFE AND KONDITOREI ($$)

www.kafeleopolds.com
Designed to be sleek and modern, this Austrian café offers dishes ranging from Veal Schnitzel to a delicious selection of salads. Leopold's also has a huge pastry selection.
🚇 C4 ✉ 3315 M Street NW ☎ 202/965-6005 🕐 Daily breakfast, lunch, dinner

MICHEL RICHARD CITRONELLE ($$$)

www.citronelledc.com
Richard is still far ahead of the pack in DC with his exquisite French/ Californian cuisine, heavenly desserts and playful

BARBECUE BATTLE

One weekend every June barbecuers from around the country gather on Pennsylvania Avenue NW between 9th and 14th streets to face off. You be the judge. Entertainment includes live rock, jazz and blues acts and cooking demonstrations.
🍴 Moderate

presentations. Jacket required for dinner.
🚇 D4 ✉ Latham Hotel, 3000 M Street NW ☎ 202/625-2150 🕐 Daily dinner 🚌 Foggy Bottom, then bus 35 or 38B

MIE N YU ($$)

www.mienyu.com
This gorgeous Asian-themed restaurant has won multiple awards for its wine list and cooking, which spans the Far and Middle East and uses only all-natural and sustainable ingredients from local farms.
🚇 C4 ✉ 3125 M Street, NW (between Wisconsin and 31st on the north side of M Street) ☎ 202/333-6122 🕐 Daily dinner; Fri–Sun brunch, lunch. Lounge Sun–Thu 5pm–2am, Fri–Sat 5pm–3am 🚌 Foggy Bottom

NEYLA ($$$)

www.neyla.com
This "Mediterranean Grill" draws a beautiful and powerful crowd with its vibrant dining room.
🚇 C4 ✉ 3206 N Street NW ☎ 202/333-6353 🕐 Daily dinner

PIZZERIA PARADISO ($)

www.eatyourpizza.com
The stone, wood-burning oven is the heart of this restaurant, which pumps out the best Neapolitan pizza in town.
🚇 C4 ✉ 3282 M Street NW ☎ 202/337-1245 🕐 Mon–Thu 11.30–11.00, Fri–Sat 11.30am–midnight, Sun 12–10

Mostly residential, Northwest Washington is home to shady streets and most of DC's embassies and mansions. With more than its fair share of restaurants and bars, it's also a popular nighttime destination.

Northwest Washington

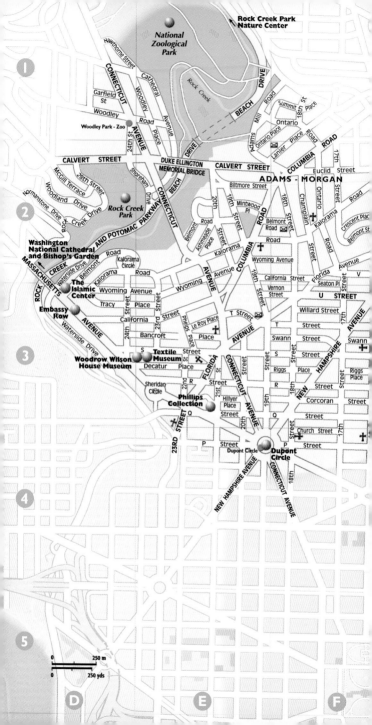

Rock Creek Park
Nature Center

National
Zoological Park

1

Rock Creek

BEACH DRIVE

CONNECTICUT

Hawthorne Street

Garfield St

Cathedral

Woodley

Woodley Park - Zoo

24th
AVENUE

Woodley
Road

Avenue

Place

DUKE ELLINGTON
MEMORIAL BRIDGE

CALVERT STREET

CALVERT STREET

Adams Mill

Ontario

Summit St
S Place

Ontario Place

Lanier Place

COLUMBIA
ROAD

17th

2

McGill Terrace

Normanstone Drive

Woodland Drive

28th Street

Rock Creek Drive

Rock Creek Park

Shoreham Drive

BEACH

CONNECTICUT

AND POTOMAC PARKWAY

ADAMS - MORGAN

Euclid Street

Biltmore Street

Champlain

18th Street

Ontario
Street

Road

Kalorama

Crescent Plac

Belmont St

Mintwood
Pl

20th
Street

19th
Street

Belmont
Road

Belmont
Road

Road

Kalorama

COLUMBIA

Ashmeade
Place

Washington
National Cathedral
and Bishop's Garden

CREEK

ROCK

MASSACHUSETTS

Waterside Drive

Belmont

Road

Kalorama
Circle

Kalorama
Road

Wyoming Avenue

19th
Street

California Street

Florida

V

Seaton Pl

Avenue

17th
Street

U STREET

AVENUE

The
Islamic
Center

Wyoming Avenue

Wyoming AVENUE

Vernon
Street

Willard Street

Street

Swann

Street

Swann

Tracy

Street

23rd Street

AVENUE

T

Street

T Street

NEW

Riggs
Place

Riggs Place

Church Street

17th

3

Embassy Row

AVENUE

California

Bancroft

Le Roy Place

Phillips
Place

Street

Swann

Street

Street

HAMPSHIRE

Waterside Drive

24th
Street

23rd Street

Textile
Museum

Street

S

Street

Riggs

Street

Woodrow Wilson
House Museum

S

Decatur

Place

FLORIDA

T St

R Street

19th

18th
Street

Corcoran

Street

Sheridan
Circle

22nd St

2nd St

1st St

Hillyer
Place

Street

Q

Street

Street

Phillips
Collection

Q
Street

20th

Street

P

4

23RD STREET

Q
Street

P Street

Street

Dupont Circle

Dupont
Circle

18th

P
Street

NEW HAMPSHIRE AVENUE

CONNECTICUT AVENUE

NEW HAMPSHIRE AVENUE

CONNECTICUT AVENUE

5

0   250 m

0   250 yds

D   **E**   **F**

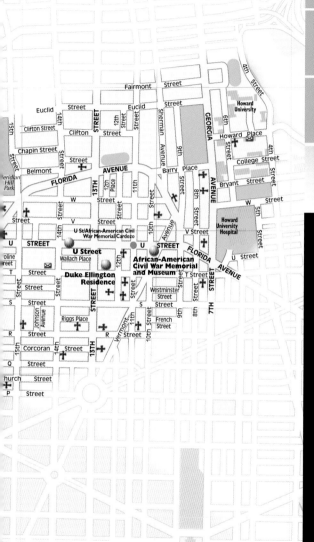

Fairmont Street

Euclid Street
Euclid Street

Clifton Street
Clifton Street

Chapin Street
Street

Belmont

FLORIDA AVENUE

Howard University

GEORGIA AVENUE

Howard Place

College Street

Bryant Street

W Street

Howard University Hospital

U Street

FLORIDA AVENUE

U St/African-American Civil War Memorial/Cardozo

U Street

U STREET

African-American Civil War Memorial and Museum

Wallach Place

Duke Ellington Residence

Westminster Street

T Street

French Street

Riggs Place

Johnson Avenue

Corcoran Street

Q Street

P Street

Meridian Hill Park

G

H

National Zoological Park

Exploring panda (left) and a male lion relaxing at the National Zoological Park (right)

THE BASICS

www.nationalzoo.si.edu
- E1
- 3001 Connecticut Avenue NW
- 202/633–4800
- Grounds daily 6–6 (until 8pm in summer). Animal buildings Apr–end Oct daily 10–6; Nov–end Mar daily 10–5
- Free. Parking charge
- Snack bars
- Woodley Park–Zoo

HIGHLIGHTS

- Tai Shan, the new Panda
- Amazonia
- Orangutans on the "O line"
- Bird House
- Hippopotami
- Lions, tigers and cheetahs
- Kid's Farm

Founded in 1889, this 163-acre (66ha) park, one of America's finest zoos, is home to more than 2,400 animals of over 400 species. Come here to watch monkeys swing, seals jump and crocs swim.

Before elephants and donkeys A national zoo was the vision of William Hornaday, who was a taxidermist at the Smithsonian. Hornaday opened a "trial zoo," packed with animals including bears and bison, right outside the Smithsonian Castle on the Mall. Not surprisingly, Congress soon approved a site a little farther away in Rock Creek Park, which the zoo still calls home. Plans for the spot were drawn up by the Secretary of the Smithsonian, Hornaday, and Frederick Law Olmsted Jr., son of the designer of Central Park in New York. When Hornaday was not chosen as the first director of the zoo, he left and founded the Bronx Zoo.

America's park More than two million visitors a year come to see the zoo's massive collection of flora and fauna. At the moment, the zoo's most popular inhabitant is Tai Shan, the first panda cub to survive more than a few days at the zoo. Tai Shan was born to Mei Xiang and Tian Tian, who replaced the famous Ling-Ling and Hsing-Hsing, gifts from China after President Nixon's (1913–94) historic visit. Visitors also come to see the big cats, the "O line," which allows orangutans to swing freely, Amazonia and the Reptile Discovery Center, where the first Komodo dragon born outside of Indonesia lives. The zoo is also home to hippopotami, giraffes, elephants and monkeys.

Phillips Collection

The former home of Duncan Phillips, housing the Phillips Collection, a gallery of modern art

This collection in the former house of Duncan Phillips was one of America's first museums of modern art and is still internationally renowned for its collection of Impressionist and Post-Impressionist paintings.

Duncan Phillips In 1918, after the premature death of his parents, Phillips established a gallery in their honor in a room of his Georgian revival home. Over the years, Phillips and his wife Marjorie, a painter, continued to buy art with a keen eye. The size of his collection grew to more than 2,000 works, including some selections that were risky at the time—Georgia O'Keeffe, Mark Rothko and Pierre Bonnard. They also bought August Renior's *Luncheon of the Boating Party* for a record price of $125,000. In 1930, Phillips moved out and the collection took over. Phillips continued to direct the gallery until his death in 1966. A new building has added a huge area of gallery space and an auditorium. There is also a good museum shop selling gifts and books.

Drawing connections Phillips believed strongly in an art lineage—that artists were clearly influenced by their predecessors as they were in turn by those who came before them. A recent exhibit highlighted the work of Brett Weston, the son of Edward Weston. The permanent collection contains works by Cubist Georges Braque, Piet Mondrian, Paul Klee, Pablo Picasso, Monet, Degas, Matisse, van Gogh, Cézanne and many well-known American artists.

THE BASICS

www.phillipscollection.org

✚ E3

✉ 1600 21st Street NW

☎ 202/387-2151

🕐 Tue–Sat 10–5 (Thu until 8.30), Sun 11–6. Closed public hols

💰 Permanent collection: free weekdays, moderate to expensive Sat–Sun. Price varies for temporary exhibitions

♿ Excellent 🍴 Café

Ⓜ Dupont Circle

❓ Tue–Fri short tours at noon, Sat–Sun noon, Thu 6pm. Concerts in the Music Room Sep–end May Sun 5pm

HIGHLIGHTS

● *Luncheon of the Boating Party*, Auguste Renoir
● *The Way to the Citadel*, Paul Klee
● *Repentant Peter*, El Greco
● *Entrance to the Public Garden at Arles*, Vincent van Gogh
● *Dancers at the Bar*, Edgar Degas
● *The Terrace*, Pierre Bonnard

TOP 25

Rock Creek Park

Rock Creek Park in fall (left) and Rock Creek (right)

THE BASICS

www.nps.gov/rocr

➕ D2

✉ Nature Center, 5200 Glover Road NW

☎ 202/895–6000; Nature Center 202/895–6070

🕐 Nature Center Wed–Sun 9–5. Grounds daylight hours

🎟 Free

🚇 Woodley Park–Zoo

HIGHLIGHTS

- Rock Creek Parkway
- Running and biking trails
- Carter Barron
- Amphitheater
- Nature Center and Planetarium
- Peirce Mill
- The Old Stone House
- Extensive hiking trails

A geological rift that slices through northwest DC, Rock Creek Park is unique as one of the few metropolitan parks to be shaped mainly by its geology, not the work of man. Offering a welcome respite from summer heat, this park has long been popular among Washingtonians.

Park of Presidents In 1890, President Benjamin Harrison (1833–1901) signed a bill establishing Rock Creek Park as one of the first national parks. The area, over 1,700 acres (687ha), was acquired for a little more than $1 million. While in office, President Theodore Roosevelt, an avid naturalist, would often spend his afternoons hiking in unmarked sections of the park with the French Ambassador, making sure to return after dark so that his appearance "would scandalize no one." Rock Creek Parkway, on the National Registry of Historic Places, was built from 1923 to 1936. During his presidency, Woodrow Wilson would have his driver drop him off in the park with the woman he was courting and then pick them up farther down the road.

Playground of Washingtonians At twice the size of Central Park, Rock Creek Park has enough room for everyone. A paved bike trail leads from the Lincoln Memorial all the way to Maryland, and Beach Drive north of Military Road is closed to motor traffic on the weekends during the day. The park is full of hiking trails and picnic areas, most of which are delineated on park maps. There is also a golf course, tennis courts and horse center.

More to See

AFRICAN-AMERICAN CIVIL WAR MEMORIAL AND MUSEUM

www.afroamcivilwar.org

This museum tells the story of the 209,145 African-Americans who fought to abolish slavery in the American Civil War. Edward Hamilton's bronze memorial, two blocks east, was dedicated in 1999.

🞣 G3 ✉ 1200 U Street NW ☎ 202/667–2667 🕙 Museum Mon–Fri 10–5, Sat 10–2; Memorial 24 hours 🚇 U Street–African-American Civil War Memorial 🎟 Free

BISHOP'S GARDEN

Built around European ruins and a statue of the Prodigal Son, this gem of a garden at Washington National Cathedral contains herbs, boxwood, magnolia trees and tea roses.

🞣 B1 ✉ Wisconsin and Massachusetts Avenues NW ☎ 202/537–6200 🕙 Daily dawn–dusk 🚇 Tenley Town; 30 series bus south 🎟 Free

DUPONT CIRCLE

During the warmer months, the grassy areas in the center of the Circle team with sunbathers, gawkers and chess-masters. Home to the rich and famous during the early 20th century, Dupont is now home to a younger (but still rich) crowd and is the epicenter of the city's gay community.

🞣 E4 🚇 Dupont Circle

EDWARD KENNEDY "DUKE" ELLINGTON RESIDENCE

Though born at 1217 22nd Street NW, "Duke" Ellington (1899–1974) grew up on this street and took piano lessons nearby.

🞣 G3 ✉ 1805–1816 13th Street NW 🕙 Not open to public 🚇 U Street–Cardozo

EMBASSY ROW

Many of the capital's most beautiful embassies line Massachusetts Avenue north of Dupont Circle. In procession, you pass the Beaux Arts Indonesian Embassy built in 1902; the Estonian Embassy, which bears striking resemblance to the buildings in Tallinn; Sheridan Circle; and the French Renaissance Embassy of Cameroon.

🞣 D3 🚇 Dupont Circle

Fountain commemorating Samuel Francis du Pont in central Dupont Circle

THE ISLAMIC CENTER

From this mosque and cultural center built in 1957 calls to the faithful emanate from a 162ft (49m) minaret. The inside is adorned with Persian carpets, ebony and ivory carvings, stained glass and mosaics.

✚ D3 ✉ 2551 Massachusetts Avenue NW ☎ 202/332–8343 🕐 Cultural Center: daily 10–5; mosque: between prayer times 🚇 Dupont Circle

TEXTILE MUSEUM

www.textilemusem.org

It may sound drab but this museum houses a stunning collection of clothing, carpets, and Islamic textiles.

✚ E3 ✉ 2320 S Street NW ☎ 202/ 667–0441 🕐 Tue–Sat 10–5, Sun 1–5 🚇 Dupont Circle 🏷 Free (suggested donation $5)

U STREET

Predating Harlem as an urban gathering place for African Americans, U Street was a mecca for jazz musicians, including Billie Holliday and Louis Armstrong. The 1968 riots dulled the area's shine, but it is now experiencing an intense revival and one of the fastest growth rates in the city.

✚ G3 ✉ U Street between 10th and 15th streets 🚇 U Street–African-American Civil War Memorial–Cardozo

WASHINGTON NATIONAL CATHEDRAL

www.nationalcathedral.org

This Gothic cathedral, the sixth largest in the world, has held state funerals and Presidential prayer services. Bring binoculars to check out the gargoyles.

✚ B1 ✉ Wisconsin and Massachusetts avenues NW ☎ 202/537–6200 🕐 Mon–Fri 10–5.30, Sat 10–4.30, Sun 1–4 🚇 Tenley Town; 30 series bus south 🏷 Free

WOODROW WILSON HOUSE MUSEUM

www.woodrowwilsonhouse.org

Woodrow Wilson lived here with his wife from 1921 until his death in 1924. This is Washington DC's only presedential museum.

✚ D3 ✉ 2340 S Street ☎ 202/387–4062 🕐 Tue–Sun 10–4 🚇 Dupont Circle 🏷 Inexpensive, under 7 free

The minaret of The Islamic Center

Cosmopolitan Washington

Dupont's tree-shaded streets and Circle offer a glimpse of both young, hip DC and elegant, old-fashioned architecture.

DISTANCE: 2.5 miles (4km) **ALLOW:** 1 hour 30 minutes

START

DUPONT CIRCLE (▷ 87)
🚇 E4 🔵 Dupont Circle

END

DUPONT CIRCLE (▷ 87)
🚇 E4 🔵 Dupont Circle

① Begin at Dupont Circle Metro's Q Street exit. Go east on Q past Thomas F. Schneider's town houses (1889–92) and the Cairo Apartments (1894).

② Turn right on 17th Street, a bustling strip in the warmer months. Take another right on Church Street, which passes some lovely Dupont town houses. Turn left on 18th Street and then right on P Street.

③ Before you cross over into the Circle, look right to check out the Patterson House, where President Coolidge lived while the White House was being renovated. Many photos of Charles Lindbergh show him waving from this balcony.

④ Pass into the Circle with the Dupont Memorial Fountain, designed by Lincoln Memorial sculptor Daniel French. Head southwest (roughly left) on New Hampshire Avenue to 1307, the "Brewmaster's Castle."

⑧ Turn left onto Decatur Place, left onto Florida Avenue and continue to Connecticut Avenue; Dupont Circle Metro is down the hill.

⑦ Past Sheridan Circle, turn right on S Street, which runs along a hilltop park. Walk down the Decatur stairs on your right.

⑥ On Massachusetts you will pass the Phillips Collection (▷ 85) and the Anderson House, home of the Society of the Cincinnati.

⑤ Turn right onto 20th, then left onto Massachusetts. On the left is the Walsh Mansion, purchased in 1951 by Indonesia for a tenth of the $3 million it cost to build in 1903.

Shopping

BEADAZZLED
www.bedazzled.net
A playground for those who make their own jewelry, this store stocks a massive collection of beads, tools and books.
🕂 E3 ✉ 1507 Connecticut Avenue NW ☎ 202/265–2323 🕔 Mon–Sat 10–8, Sun 11–6 🚇 Dupont Circle

BETSY FISHER
www.betsyfisher.com
Carrying designers like Nanette Lapore and Diane von Furstenberg, along with a few local designers, Betsy Fisher draws women young, old and in between.
🕂 F4 ✉ 1224 Connecticut Avenue NW ☎ 202/785–1975 🕔 Mon–Wed 10–7, Thu–Fri 10–8, Sat 10–6, Sun 12–4 🚇 Dupont Circle

BLUE MERCURY
www.bluemercury.com
Aside from its hard-to-match selection of hair- and skin-care products, Blue Mercury also provides Diptyque candles and a number of spa treatments.
🕂 E3 ✉ 1619 Connecticut Avenue NW ☎ 202/462–1300 🕔 Mon–Sat 10–8, Sun 12–6 🚇 Dupont Circle

CALVERT WOODLEY LIQUORS
In business for more than two decades, Calvert Woodley stocks DC's largest selection of wine as well as a range of fantastic cheese.
🕂 D1 ✉ 4339 Connecticut Avenue NW ☎ 202/966–4400 🕔 Mon–Sat 10–8.30 🚇 Woodley Park–Zoo

CARBON
www.carbondc.com
A shoe store for the hip male and female carries Tsubo and Mis Mozz, among others.
🕂 G3 ✉ 2643 Connecticut Avenue NW ☎ 202/232–6645 🕔 Mon–Sat 12–7.30, Sun 12–5 🚇 Woodley Zoo

COFFEE AND THE WORKS
This narrow store is packed with high-end and some hard-to-find kitchenware, along with a good selection of tea and coffee.
🕂 E3 ✉ 1627 Connecticut Avenue NW ☎ 202/483–8050 🕔 Mon–Sat 12–7.30, Sun 12–5 🚇 Dupont Circle

GOOD WOOD
www.goodwooddc.com
This friendly U Street shop carries high-quality, reasonably priced furniture, along with other things for the house and vintage jewelry.
🕂 G3 ✉ 1428 U Street NW ☎ 202/986–3640 🕔 Thu 5–9pm, Fri–Sat 11–7, Sun 11–5 🚇 U Street–African-American Civil War Memorial–Cardozo

HEMPHILL FINE ARTS
In up-and-coming Logan Circle, this large gallery stocks an impressive array of American artists.
🕂 G4 ✉ 1515 14th Street NW, 3rd floor ☎ 202/234–5601 🕔 Thu–Sat 10–5 🚇 U Street–African-American Civil War Memorial–Cardozo

KRAMERBOOKS AND AFTERWORDS CAFÉ
www.kramers.com
This intimate bookstore/bar/brunch spot/late night hangout is always buzzing with activity—from those browsing for their next read among the well-picked selection to those looking for their next date.
🕂 E3 ✉ 1517 Connecticut Avenue NW ☎ 202/387–1400 🕔 Sun–Thu 7.30am–1am, Fri–Sat 24 hours 🚇 Dupont Circle

LAMBDA RISING
This playful bookstore is world famous and a bisexual, gay, lesbian, transgender landmark.
🕂 E3 ✉ 1625 Connecticut Avenue NW ☎ 202/462–6969 🕔 Sun–Thu 10–10,

Fri–Sat 10–midnight
Ⓜ Dupont Circle

MEEPS FASHIONETTE

This town house stocks well-priced men's and women's vintage clothing, along with a "local focus" section.
➕ F3 ✉ 2104 18th Street NW ☎ 202/265–6546 Ⓖ Tue–Sat 12–7, Sun 12–5 Ⓜ U Street–African-American Civil War Memorial–Cardozo

MISS PIXIE'S

Stocked with low-price and well-picked antiques and vintage home furnishings, Miss Pixie's is popular among a young, hip crowd.
➕ F2 ✉ 1626 14th Street NW ☎ 202/232–8171 Ⓖ Tue–Sun 12–7 Ⓜ Dupont Circle

MULÉH

Half Balinese and Filipino home furnishings, this high-end store specializes in natural materials.
➕ G3 ✉ 1831 14th Street NW ☎ 202/667–3440 Ⓖ Tue–Sat 11–7, Sun 12–5 Ⓜ U Street–African-American Civil War Memorial–Cardozo

NANA

Unique and affordable, Nana's deftly matches cool new styles with timeless older ones.
➕ F3 ✉ 1528 U Street NW ☎ 202/667–6955 Ⓖ Tue–Sat 12–7, Sun 12–5 Ⓜ U Street–Cardozo

PINK NOVEMBER

Intended for those who think themselves

fabulous, this fantasy experience stocks one-of-a-kind women's clothing and accessories.
➕ G3 ✉ 1534 U Street NW ☎ 202/333–1121 Ⓖ Mon–Sat 10–8, Sun 12–6 Ⓜ U Street–African-American Civil War Memorial–Cardozo

PROPER TOPPER

www.propertopper.com
Fashionable head wear, of course, is the main draw here, but also come for myriad accessories and home decor.
➕ F4 ✉ 1350 Connecticut Avenue NW ☎ 202/842–3055 Ⓖ Mon–Fri 10–8, Sat 10–7, Sun 12–6 Ⓜ Dupont Circle

RIZIK BROTHERS

www.riziks.com
Rizik's is Washington's go-to spot for gowns. From evening wear through bridal wear to casual day clothes and coats and jackets, Rizik's has been around for nearly a century and continues to please. There's a good range of accessories, too.
➕ F4 ✉ 1100 Connecticut Avenue NW ✉ 202/223–4050 Ⓖ Mon–Sat 9–6, Thu 9–8 Ⓜ Dupont Circle

---

TREASURE HUNTING

Georgetown, Adams-Morgan, Dupont Circle and the 7th Street art corridor are abundantly supplied with galleries, boutiques and specialist stores.

SECONDI

Washington's top stop for secondhand clothes, Secondi is no thrift store–despite the prices. Brands include Marc Jacobs, Prada and Louis Vuitton.
➕ E3 ✉ 1702 Connecticut Avenue NW, 2nd floor ☎ 202/667–1122 Ⓖ Mon–Tue 11–6, Wed–Fri 11–7, Sat 11–6, Sun 1–5 Ⓜ Dupont Circle

SECOND STORY BOOKS

If used books are your passion, start here. If you don't find your treasure on the rows of shelves, it may be in Second Story's warehouse.
➕ E4 ✉ 2000 P Street NW ☎ 202/659–8884 Ⓖ Daily 10–10 Ⓜ Dupont Circle

TABLETOP

www.tabletopdc.com
Sleek retro housewares are the calling card of this location. Items are well designed and priced as such, but be sure not to forget the bargain area in the back.
➕ E3 ✉ 1608 20th Street NW ☎ 202/387–7117 Ⓖ Mon–Sat 12–8, Sun 12–6 Ⓜ Dupont Circle

THOMAS PINK

High-end, yet inviting, this branch of the English shirtmaker caters to both men and women.
➕ F4 ✉ 1127 Connecticut Avenue NW ☎ 202/223–5390 Ⓖ Mon–Fri 10–7, Sat 10–6, Sun 12–5 Ⓜ Dupont Circle

Entertainment and Nightlife

9:30 CLUB
www.930.com
See the most popular non-stadium acts—like the Brazilian Girls, Wilco and Blackalicious—take the stage at this simple, well-designed club.
➕ H2 ✉ 815 V Street NW ☎ 202/265-0930 🕐 Daily from 9.30pm 🚇 U Street–African-American Civil War Memorial–Cardozo

CAFÉ CITRON
www.cafecitrondc.com
Live Latin music and well-priced mohitos keep this spot hot, even on DC's coldest nights.
➕ F4 ✉ 1343 Connecticut Avenue NW ☎ 202/530-8844 🕐 Daily 10am–midnight 🚇 Dupont Circle

CHI-CHA LOUNGE
A plush lounge filled with sofas and hip young professionals, Chi-Cha offers live Latin jazz, Andean tapas, a tasty namesake drink and hookahs.
➕ F3 ✉ 1624 U Street NW ☎ 202/234-8400 🕐 Daily 5pm–2am 🚇 U Street–Cardozo, Dupont Circle

EIGHTEENTH STREET LOUNGE (ESL)
www.eighteenthstreetlounge.com
This multilevel, sofa-filled house party is popular among Washington's most chic. To get in here you need to dress well.
➕ F4 ✉ 1212 18th Street NW ☎ 202/466-3922 🕐 Tue–Thu 5.30pm–2am,
Fri 5.30pm–3am, Sat 9.30pm–3am, Sun (9.30pm–2am. No admittance 1 hour before closing; cover charge 🚇 Dupont Circle

HR-57
Doubling as a nonprofit cultural center, this unpretentious jazz club serves up talented local artists along with tasty bites such as fried chicken and collard greens.
➕ G3 ✉ 1610 14th Street NW ☎ 202/667-3700 🕐 Thu–Sat 9pm–1am. Jam sessions Wed, Thu, Sun 7–11 🚇 U Street–Cardozo

MARVIN
www.marvindc.com
Eighteen Street Lounge's more accessible sister offers a selection of Belgian beer and a cozy dancing floor.

ADAMS-MORGAN

By far the liveliest and most eclectic nightlife scene in town is in Adams-Morgan. The strip, wall-to-wall bars and restaurants on 18th Street NW from Kalorama Road to Columbia Avenue and then spilling east and west, has something for everyone. Just to name a few: Bourbon, a whisky bar; Habana Village with salsa dancing and mohitos; Madam's Organ with nightly live music was one of Playboy's "best bars in America;" Rumba Cafe with live Latin music; and Toledo Lounge, a straight-up bar.

➕ G3 ✉ 2007 14th Street NW ☎ 202/797-7171 🚇 U Street–Cardozo

RUSSIA HOUSE
Scores of bottles of chilled vodka, ranging from the popular to the bizarre, lie in wait at this plush, red lounge.
➕ E3 ✉ 1800 Connecticut Avenue NW ☎ 202/234-9433 🕐 Mon–Thu 5pm–midnight, Fri 5pm–2am, Sat 6pm–2am, Sun 6pm–midnight 🚇 Dupont Circle

SALOON
The Saloon prohibits standing and the ordering of martinis, but regulars find the select beer list and the conversation inviting.
➕ E3 ✉ 1207 U Street NW ☎ 202/462-2640 🕐 Tue–Thu 11am–1am, Fri 11am–2am, Sat 2pm–2am 🚇 U Street–Cardozo

STUDIO THEATRE
www.studiotheatre.org
This independent company produces an eclectic season of classic and offbeat plays.
➕ G4 ✉ 1501 14th Street NW ☎ 202/332-3300 🚇 Dupont Circle

TABARD INN
www.tabardinn.com
This hotel's warm sitting room has sofas, wood paneling, a fireplace and Jazz on Sunday nights.
➕ F4 ✉ 1739 N Street NW ☎ 202/331-8528 🕐 Tue–Sat 6–10.30, Sun 6–10 🚇 Dupont Circle

Restaurants

PRICES

Prices are approximate,
based on a 3-course
meal for one person.
$$$ over $50
$$ $30–$50
$ under $30

AMSTERDAM FALAFELSHOP ($)

Falafel and fries may be
the only thing on the
menu here, but dozens
of fresh toppings—sauces,
salads and pickles—make
the difference.
⊞ F2 ✉ 2425 18th Street
NW ☎ 202/234-1969
🕐 Daily 11am-very late
Ⓜ Woodley Park

BEN'S CHILI BOWL ($)

www.benschilibowl.com
A U Street institution,
Ben's Chili Bowl sells
burgers, hot dogs and
fries to a late-night crowd,
most of whom get their
munchy coated in chili.
⊞ G3 ✉ 1213 U Street NW
☎ 202/667-0909
🕐 Mon–Sat breakfast, lunch,
dinner, late night; Sun lunch,
dinner Ⓜ U Street–Cardozo

BUKOM CAFÉ ($)

www.bukomcom
Sunny African pop music,
and a spicy West Africa
menu filled with goat,
lamb, chicken and
vegetable. Open late;
live music nightly.
⊞ F2 ✉ 2442 18th Street
NW ☎ 202/265-4600
🕐 Daily dinner Ⓜ Woodley
Park–Zoo, then bus 92 or 96

BUSBOYS AND POETS ($–$$)

www.busboysandpoets.com
A comfortable and hip
coffee shop, bookstore,
restaurant, art gallery and
performance space, Bus-
boys has quickly become
a gathering spot for this
neighborhood.
⊞ G3 ✉ 2021 14th Street
NW ☎ 202/387-7638
🕐 Sun 9am–midnight,
Mon–Thu 8am–midnight,
Fri 8am–midnight, Sat 9am–
midnight Ⓜ U Street–Cardozo

THE DINER ($)

Solid diner standards,
along with cocktails, are
served in this hipster
hangout.
⊞ F2 ✉ 2453 18th Street
NW ☎ 202/232-8800
🕐 Sun–Thu 6am–midnight,
Fri–Sat 6am–1am Ⓜ Dupont
Circle, then bus 42

MULTICULTURAL

The city's most multicultural
neighborhood is crowded,
bustling and filled with ethnic
restaurants. A walk along
18th Street leads past:
Bukom Café and **The Diner**
(see main entries this page);
Fasika's (Ethiopian
✉ 2447 18th Street
☎ 202/797-7673);
Little Fountain Café
(International ✉ 2339 18th
Street ☎ 202/462-8100);
Meskerem (Ethiopian
✉ 2434 18th Street
☎ 202/462-4100);
Mezè (▷ 94).

HANK'S OYSTER BAR ($$)

www.hanksdc.com
This narrow, lively
sea-food stop serves up
simple, yet skillful, dishes
that draw your attention
to the finest, high-quality
ingredients.
⊞ F3 ✉ 1624 Q Street NW
☎ 202/462-4265
🕐 Mon–Fri dinner; Sat–Sun
lunch, dinner
Ⓜ Dupont Circle

INDIQUE ($$)

www.indique.com
Modern Indian food
(served as tapas or
entrées), creative
cocktails and an icy cool
setting draw in a sophisticated crowd.
⊞ Off map at D1 ✉ 3512
Connecticut Avenue NW
☎ 202/244-6600 🕐 Mon–
Sat lunch, daily dinner
Ⓜ Cleveland Park

KOMI ($$$)

Young chef Johnny Monis
draws foodies from all
over the city with his
basic, yet inspired, dishes
crafted with fantastic
ingredients. The cuisine
has Greek influences.
⊞ F3 ✉ 1509 17th Street
NW ☎ 202/332-9200
🕐 Tue–Sat dinner Ⓜ Dupont
Circle

LAURIOL PLAZA ($)

www.lauriolplaza.com
Extremely popular among
young Hill staff for its
open-air top floor and
slushy margaritas,
Lauriol's food isn't too
bad, either.

🗺 F3 ✉ 1835 18th Street NW ☎ 202/387-0035 🕐 Daily lunch, dinner 🚇 Dupont Circle

LEBANESE TAVERNA ($–$$)

www.lebanesetaverna.com
Specializing in Lebanese *meze*, this popular restaurant is known for its warm hospitality.
🗺 E1 ✉ 2641 Connecticut Avenue NW ☎ 202/265-8681 🕐 Daily lunch, dinner 🚇 Woodley Park–Zoo

MADJET ($–$$)

Dukem next door may get more traffic, but this small, intimate restaurant serves the best Ethiopian food in town.
🗺 G3 ✉ 1102 U Street NW ☎ 202/265-1952 🕐 Daily lunch, dinner 🚇 U Street–Cardozo

MARVELOUS MARKET ($)

www.marvelousmarket.com
Although a little pricey, Marvelous provides a wonderful array of picnic supplies, perfect for those wishing to dine in the Circle alfresco.
🗺 E3 ✉ 1511 Connecticut Avenue NW ☎ 202/332-3690 🕐 Mon–Fri 7am–9pm, Sat 8.30-8.30, Sun 8.30-7 🚇 Dupont Circle

MEZÈ ($–$$)

www.mezedc.com
This cool Turkish spot consistently churns out tasty *mezes* and offers a roomy patio for the warmer months.

🗺 F2 ✉ 2437 18th Street ☎ 202/797-0017 🕐 Mon–Thu 5.30pm–1.30am, Fri 5.30pm–2.30am, Sat 11am–2.30am, Sun 11am–1.30am 🚇 Woodley Park–Zoo

NORA ($$$)

www.noras.com
The nation's first restaurant to be certified organic, Nora offers a market menu of free-range meats and local seafood in a dining room beautifully decorated with Amish quilts.
🗺 E3 ✉ 2132 Florida Avenue NW ☎ 202/462-5143 🕐 Mon–Sat dinner 🚇 Dupont Circle

PALENA ($$$)

www.palenarestaurant.com
Two former White House chefs created this informal, but first-class, restaurant that serves Italian in the more moderately priced café and high-end American in the back.
🗺 Off map at D1 ✉ 3529 Connecticut Avenue NW ☎ 202/537-9250 🕐 Tue–Sat dinner 🚇 Cleveland Park

LATE NIGHT EATS

There are many restaurants in town that cater to the late-night crowd and they typically serve outstanding nosh. If you've got the munchies past midnight, try The Diner (▷ 93), Kramerbooks and Afterwords Café (▷ 90), Ben's Chili Bowl (▷ 93) or Five Guys (▷ 31, 80).

SUSHI TARO ($$)

www.sushitaro.com
This sushi powerhouse always has three grades of tuna on hand, along with a large selection of ultrafresh and hard-to-find seafood.
🗺 F4 ✉ 1503 17th Street NW ☎ 202/462-8999 🕐 Mon–Fri lunch, dinner; Sat dinner 🚇 Dupont Circle

TEAISM ($)

This simple teahouse offers an eclectic collection of Asian-inspired dishes, such as *palak paneer* and even a turkey sandwich with nori and wasabi mayonnaise.
🗺 E3 ✉ 2009 R Street NW ☎ 202/667-3827 🕐 Daily breakfast, lunch, dinner 🚇 Dupont Circle

THAI CHEF ($)

The decor may be common, but this kitchen puts out some of the best Thai food in town.
🗺 E3 ✉ 1712 Connecticut Avenue NW ☎ 202/234-5698 🕐 Daily lunch, dinner 🚇 Dupont Circle

WELL-DRESSED BURRITO ($)

www.welldressedburrito.com
This lunch spot has been churning out freshly prepared Mexican takeout for more than two decades. The "well-dressed," a large, inexpensive burrito, changes daily.
🗺 E4 ✉ 1220 19th Street NW ☎ 202/293-0515 🕐 Mon–Fri lunch 🚇 Dupont Circle

Suburban congressional staff, tired of traveling all the way into the city for food and entertainment, are spending their money at home instead, spurring quick growth in areas just outside the District.

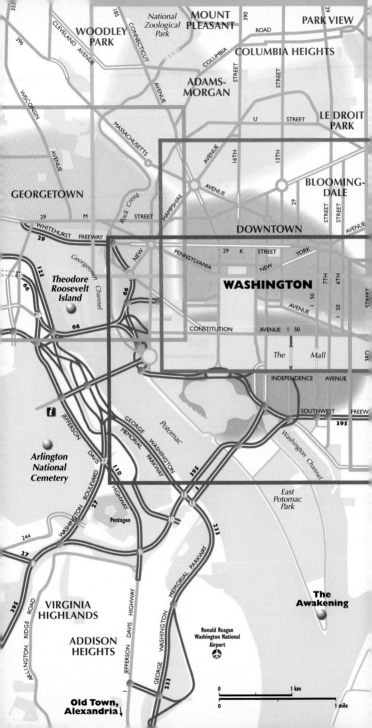

Arlington National Cemetery

HIGHLIGHTS

- Kennedy graves
- Tomb of the Unknowns
- Custis-Lee Mansion
- L'Enfant's grave
- USS *Marine* Memorial
- Shuttle *Challenger*
- Astronauts Memorial
- Changing of the Guard at the Tomb of the Unknowns

TIP

- Remember that many visit to pay respect to dead loved ones. Dress appropriately and keep an eye on your children.

The national cemetery since 1883, Arlington contains the most visited grave in the country, that of John F. Kennedy. Rows and rows of white crosses commemorate the war dead and national heroes with dignity.

Lest we forget Veterans from every American war are interred here on the land of General Robert E. Lee's (1807–70) "Arlington House." Those who fought and died before the Civil War were moved here after 1900. Perhaps the most famous soldiers to be buried here are those that have not yet been named. The Tomb of the Unknowns contains remains of a World War I, World War II and Korean War soldier. A soldier from the Vietnam War was disinterred in 1998 after DNA evidence conclusively identified him. Other memorials

Clockwise from left: Mast of Battleship Maine surrounded by gravestones in Arlington National Cemetery; Changing of the Guard at the Tomb of the Unknowns; the rooftops of the city of Washington, viewed from the hillside of the Cemetery; visitors among the blossom-covered trees and graves

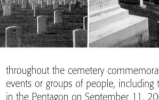

throughout the cemetery commemorate particular events or groups of people, including those killed in the Pentagon on September 11, 2001, and those aboard the Space Shuttle *Columbia* that crashed in 2003. Sentries from the Third US Infantry guard the tomb 24 hours a day and perform the Changing of the Guard ceremony.

White markers and a flame Under an eternal flame, John F. Kennedy lies next to his wife, Jacqueline Bouvier Kennedy Onassis, and two of his children who died in infancy. Nearby lies his brother, Robert Kennedy, whose grave is marked by a simple white cross and a fountain. The Greek-revival Custis-Lee Mansion sits above the Kennedy graves. Just off the house's west corner lies the grave of Pierre L'Enfant, now overlooking for eternity the Federal City that he designed.

THE BASICS

www.arlingtoncemetery.org

✚ C8

✉ Across Memorial Bridge from Lincoln Memorial

☎ 703/607–8000

🕐 Apr–end Sep daily 8–7; Oct–end Mar daily 8–5

✋ Free

♿ Excellent. Visitors with disabilities may board Tourmobile Shuttles or obtain a driving permit at the visitor center

🚇 Arlington Cemetery

🚌 Tourmobile

❓ Narrated Tourmobile Shuttle, every 20 min. Changing of the Guard: Apr–end Sep daily on the half hour; Oct–end Mar daily on the hour

Cedar Hill

The colonial-style exterior of Cedar Hill (left) and inside Frederick Douglass's home (right)

THE BASICS

www.nps.gov/frdo

✚ Off map, south of M9

✉ 1411 W Street SE

☎ 202/426–5961

🕐 Mid-Apr to mid-Oct daily 9–5; mid-Oct to mid-Apr 9–4

💲 Free

♿ Good

🚇 Anacostia, then B-2 Mt Rainer bus

🚌 By Tourmobile (mid-Jun to Labor Day daily)

☎ 202/554–5100

🚍 11th Street Bridge to Martin Luther King Avenue, right on W Street

❓ Five tours daily 9–4 (☎ 800/967–2283, www.recreation.gov)

HIGHLIGHTS

● Harriet Beecher Stowe's desk
● Portraits of Elizabeth Cady Stanton and Susan B. Anthony
● View of Washington

Built in 1854, the Italianate country house known as Cedar Hill was the last home of abolitionist Frederick Douglass. Decorative arts, libraries and family mementos provide an intimate look at his life and work.

Slave America's famous abolitionist was born into slavery in Maryland around 1818 and separated from his mother at birth. When Douglass was 12, his master's wife illegally taught him how to read. He escaped to Maryland when he was 20, becoming active in the Massachusetts anti-slavery movement. He wrote an autobiography in 1845, which became so popular that he had to flee to Europe out of fear that his former master would find out and he would be recaptured. There, British friends bought him his freedom. He lectured and published widely on anti-slavery topics, became an adviser to Lincoln, an ambassador to Haiti and a supporter of women's suffrage. When he moved into Cedar Hill, he was the first black resident of Anacostia, breaking the prohibition against "Irish, Negro, mulatto, or persons of African blood."

Viewpoint Cedar Hill, now the Frederick Douglass National Historic Site, occupies the highest point in Anacostia, with a great view of the Anacostia River and the capital. The desk at which Harriet Beecher Stowe wrote *Uncle Tom's Cabin* is one of the many objects on display inside the house. The National Park Service, which manages the site, maintains a visitor center and a bookstore specializing in African-American titles.

External light flooding the nave (left); the Byzantine-style dome and bell tower of the church (right)

Shrine of the Immaculate Conception

This is the largest church in the western hemisphere. Renowned for its mosaics, it is dedicated to Christ's mother, Mary, named Patroness of the United States by Pope Pius IX in 1847.

Construction Work began on the grounds of Catholic University in 1920. The street-level Crypt Church was completed in 1926. Construction stopped during the Great Depression and World War II, but began again in 1954. The Great Upper Church was dedicated on November 20, 1959.

American saint At the entrance to the Chapel of Our Lady Hostyn in the Crypt Church is a delicate stained-glass screen depicting scenes from the life of Saint John Neumann (1811–60), the first American to become a saint. The Crypt Church and the Great Upper Church together are home to 70 chapels and the 3-million-tile *Christ in Majesty*. The Byzantine-style dome, 237ft (72m) in height and 108ft (33m) in diameter, is decorated with symbols of the Virgin Mary picked out in gold leaf and colorful majolica tiles. The 329ft (100m) bell tower houses a 56-bell carillon cast in France and supports a 20ft (6m) gilded cross visible from a great distance. Three rose windows embellished with gold and amethyst illuminate the sanctuary, along with ranks of other windows depicting the lives of Mary, the Holy Family, saints and redeemed sinners. Sculpture includes George Carr's 37-ton marble *Universal Call to Holiness* on the south wall of the Great Upper Church, which was dedicated in 1999.

THE BASICS

www.nationalshrine.com
- Off map, north of M1
- ✉ 400 Michigan Avenue
- ☎ 202/526–8300
- 🕐 Apr–end Oct daily 7–7; Nov–end Mar daily 7–6
- 🆓 Free
- ♿ Excellent
- 🍴 Cafeteria daily 7.30–2
- Ⓜ Brookland
- ❓ Tours Mon–Sat 9–11, 1–3, Sun 1.30–4

HIGHLIGHTS
- ● Ecclesiastical sculpture
- ● Mosaics

More to See

ANACOSTIA MUSEUM AND CENTER FOR AFRICAN-AMERICAN HISTORY AND CULTURE
www.anacostia.si.edu
This Smithsonian museum showcases African-American cultural history.
🚩 Off map, south of M9 ✉ 1901 Fort Place SE ☎ 202/633–4820 🕐 Daily 10–5
🚇 Anacostia, then bus W2, W3 💲 Free

THE AWAKENING
Originally a temporary exhibit, this statue of a bearded aluminum giant emerging from the earth by J. Seward Johnson was so popular that the Park Service never removed it. The surrounding park has bike paths, tennis, swimming and golf.
🚩 Off map, south of G9 ✉ Hains Point, East Potomac Park ☎ 202/485–9880 or 202/727–6523 🕐 Daily 24 hours 💲 Free

NATIONAL ARBORETUM
www.usna.usda.gov
The Arboretum's 446 acres (180ha) invite driving, biking and hiking. The National Herb Garden, National Bonsai Collection, Azalea Walk and a display of the Capitol's original Corinthian columns are also a draw.
🚩 Off map, east of M3 ✉ 3501 New York Avenue NE ☎ 202/245–2726 🕐 Daily 8–5. Tours mid-Apr to end Oct 🚇 Weekends: shuttle from Union Station, weekdays: Stadium-Armory, then bus B2 💲 Free

OLD TOWN, ALEXANDRIA
A well-preserved colonial port town, Old Town's cobblestone streets are packed with early-American homes and taverns. Along the waterfront, tourists picnic as the boats come in.
🚩 Off map, south of E9 ✉ Old Town, Alexandria, VA 🚇 King Street

THEODORE ROOSEVELT ISLAND
www.nps.gov/this
With miles of walking trails through diverse terrain, this island in the Potomac River is a fitting memorial to the naturalist president. A 17ft-high (5m) bronze statue of Roosevelt can be found in the center of the island.
🚩 C5 🚗 Car access from northbound lane of George Washington Memorial Parkway ☎ 703/289–2500 🕐 Daily 6am–10pm

Hydrangeas in the National Arboretum

The Awakening

Excursions

FREDERICKSBURG

The 40-block National Historic District in this charming Virginia town comprises the house George Washington (1732–99) bought for his mother, a 1752 plantation, President James Monroe's (1758–1831) law offices, an early apothecary shop and the Georgian Chatham Manor, which overlooks the Rappahannock River.

Two Civil War battles were waged in and around town. You can now visit the battlefields and stroll through the nearby wilderness parks. Antiques and rare-book stores and art galleries line the streets. Start at the well-marked visitor center, which dispenses maps and advice.

THE BASICS

www.visitfred.com
Distance: 50 miles (80km)
Journey Time: 1–2 hours
🚹 706 Caroline Street
☎ 1–800/678–4748
🕐 Daily 9–5
🚆 Amtrak from Union Station
🚌 South on I–95 to exit 133A and follow signs to visitor center

MOUNT VERNON

George Washington's ancestral Virginia estate is the nation's second-most visited historic house after the White House. Washington worked this plantation's 8,000 acres (3,239ha) before he took control of the Continental Army and returned here for good after his presidency.

Washington supervised the expansion of the main house, most notably the addition of the back porch with a view over the Potomac. The mansion is built of yellow pine, painted multiple times with sand to resemble stone. The ornate interior is furnished with fine arts and memorabilia. The outbuildings re-create the spaces of a self-sufficient, 18th-century farm, including the smokehouse and laundry, outside kitchen and slave quarters. Don't miss the view of George and Martha Washington's tomb. The Ladies Association was founded in 1853 to preserve the estate.

THE BASICS

www.mountvernon.org
Distance: 17 miles (27km)
Journey Time: 40 minutes
☎ 703/780–2000
🕐 Mar, Sep–end Oct daily 9–5; Apr–end Aug 8–5; Nov–end Feb 9–4
🚆 Huntington Station, then Fairfax Connector bus
🚌 Tourmobile mid-Jun to Labor Day
🚗 Take 14th Street Bridge (toward National Airport), then south on George Washington Memorial Parkway
🚢 *Potomac Spirit* from Pier 4, 6th and Water streets SW, (☎ 202/554–8000)
💰 Expensive

Shopping

FASHION CENTER

Macy's and Nordstrom anchor the 160 stores in this Pentagon City mall. An open-air mall across the street houses an array of stores from Bed Bath & Beyond to Ann Taylor Loft to Sur La Table.
🏠 Off map at C9 ✉ 1100 S Hayes Street at Army-Navy Drive and I-395 S ☎ 703/415-2400 🕐 Mon–Sat 10–9.30, Sun 11–6 🚇 Pentagon City

FRIENDSHIP HEIGHTS

These three shopping centers are likely to fill any need. The upscale four-floor Mazza Gallerie and the Chevy Chase Pavilion across the street contain a Saks Men's Store, Filene's Basement, Pottery Barn, Williams and Sonoma and Neiman Marcus. The über-chic Collection at Chevy Chase offers Louis Vuitton, Cartier and Barneys Co-op.
🏠 Off map at A1 ✉ Wisconsin Avenue at Western Avenue 🕐 Mazza Gallerie: Mon–Fri 10–8, Sat 10–7, Sun 12–5. Chevy Chase Pavilion: Mon–Sat 9–9, Sun 11–6. Collection at Chevy Chase: hours vary 🚇 Friendship Heights

HOUSE OF MUSICAL TRADITIONS

www.hmtrad.com
Musical instruments from lap dulcimers to bag pipes are sold at this well-known location.
🏠 Off map at J1 ✉ 7040 Carrol Avenue, Takoma Park, MD ☎ 301/270–9090 🕐 Tue–Sat 11–7, Sun–Mon 11–5 🚇 Takoma

IKEA

A juggernaut of simple, inexpensive design, IKEA offers nearly everything you could want to put in your home.
🏠 Off map at M1 ✉ 10100 Baltimore Avenue, College Park, MD ☎ 301/345-6552 🕐 Mon–Sat 10–9, Sun 10–8 🚇 College Park

POTOMAC MILLS MALL

This huge outlet mall is one of Virginia's most popular destinations. Bargain shoppers enjoy Banana Republic and Polo at a discount.
🏠 Off map at A9 ✉ 2700

ROYAL TREATMENT

Political staffers don't shirk from putting in their time at work, but they also know how to be pampered. Want to see partisans reeling from a recent loss or reveling in a clear victory? Head to: Aveda (☎ 202/965–1325), Blue Mercury (▷ 90), Grooming Lounge (▷ 29), Jolie, the Day Spa (☎ 301/986-9293), or Roche Salon (☎ 202/775-0775). Many hotels, like the upscale Mandarin Oriental (▷ 112), the Ritz-Carlton (▷ 112) and the Willard (▷ 112) also have spas that give the ultimate in superb treatments.

Potomac Mills Circle, Prince William, VA, Wodbridge, VA ☎ 703/496–9330 🕐 Mon–Sat 10–9, Sun 11–6

TAKOMA UNDERGROUND

Vintage clothing, books, jewelry, furniture and knickknacks populate this subterranean space.
🏠 Off map at J1 ✉ 700 Carroll Park, Takoma Park, MD ☎ 301/270–6380 🕐 Tue–Fri 11–7, Sat 11–6, Fri 10–5 🚇 Takoma

TORPEDO FACTORY ART CENTER

Pottery, paintings, jewelry, stained glass and other works of local artists, who work in the studios of this former US Naval Torpedo Station, are on display.
🏠 Off map at F9 ✉ 105 N Union Street, Alexandria ☎ 703/838-4199 🕐 Daily 10–6 🚇 King Street, then free trolly 11.30–10 daily

TYSON'S CORNER

Tyson's Corner Center claims Nordstrom, Bloomingdale's and an AMC theater. Tyson's Galleria, across the high-way, is a little more upscale, with Saks Fifth Avenue and Chanel.
🏠 Off map at A2 ✉ 1961 Chain Bridge Road, McLean, VA ☎ 888/289–7667 or 703/847-7300 🕐 Center: Mon–Sat 10–9.30, Sun 11–6, Galleria: Mon–Sat 10–9, Sun 12–7 🚌 I-66 west to Route 7 west, then follow signs 🚇 West Falls Church Metro, then 28A, 28B or 3T bus

Entertainment and Nightlife

ARENA STAGE
www.arenastage.org
This resident company presents dynamically staged and superbly acted American theater in its three performance spaces.
🔀 H8 ✉ 1101 6th Street SW
☎ 202/488-3300
🚇 Waterfront-SEU

BIRCHMERE
www.birchmere.com
One of America's top spots to catch bluegrass and folk. Has hosted the likes of Arlo Guthrie.
🔀 Off map at D9 ✉ 3701 Mount Vernon Avenue, Alexandria, VA ☎ 703/549-7500 ⏰ Sun-Thu 6.30pm-11pm, Fri-Sat 7pm-12.30am 🚇 Pentagon City, then taxi

CONTINENTAL
This hip billiards hall is adorned with bright, retro decor and several cozy lounges, perfect for relaxing between games.
🔀 B5 ✉ 1911 North Fort Myer Drive, Arlington, VA
☎ 703/465-7675
⏰ Mon-Fri 11.30am-2am, Sat-Sun 6pm-2am 🚇 Rosslyn

LOVE THE CLUB
www.lovetheclub.com
Housed in a former warehouse in an industrial area, this elegant four-floor club is popular among local professional athletes and celebrities.
🔀 M3 ✉ 1350 Okie Street NE ☎ 202/636-9030
⏰ Fri doors open 10pm, Sat 9pm 🚌 Shuttle service from 18th and M Street NW

PUPPET COMPANY PLAYHOUSE
www.thepuppetco.org
This talented puppet troupe performs to children of all ages.
🔀 Off map at A1
✉ 7300 MacArthur Boulevard, Glen Echo, MD
☎ 301/634-5380 🚌 29

ROCK AND ROLL HOTEL
www.rockandrollhoteldc.com
A popular live-music venue that plays host to solid indie bands, and is a centerpiece of the "H Street" revival.
🔀 M5 ✉ 1353 H Street NE
☎ 202/388-7625 ⏰ Daily 8pm-late 🚇 Gallery Place, then free shuttle bus

ROUND HOUSE THEATRE
www.round-house.org
In a modern new space in Bethesda, Round

POLITICAL PUNCHLINES
Two talented troupes in town specialize in poking fun at both political parties—Capitol Steps (☎ 703/683-8330), a group of former and current Hill staffers, and Gross National Product (☎ 202/783-7212). Washington Improv Theater (WIT) (☎ 202/315-1318) and ComedySportz (☎ 703/294-5233) tend toward more traditional improv, while DC Improv (☎ 202/296-7008) is the spot to see well-known stand-up acts.

House has continued to produce an eclectic set of professional plays.
🔀 Off map at A1 ✉ 4545 East-West Highway, Bethesda, MD ☎ 240/644-1100
🚇 Bethesda

SIGNATURE THEATRE
This theater has become renowned for its sharply produced musicals, especially those of Steven Sondheim.
🔀 Off map at A9
✉ 4200 Campbell Avenue
☎ 703/820-9771
🚇 Pentagon City, then taxi

STRATHMORE
www.strathmore.org
This major music venue, just outside the beltway, is a favorite, with great acoustics. It is now home to the Baltimore Symphony Orchestra and the National Philharmonic.
🔀 Off map at A1
✉ 5301 Tuckerman Lane, North Bethesda, MD
☎ 301/581-5200
🚇 Grovesnor-Strathmore

WOLF TRAP
www.wolftrap.org
The only National Park devoted to the performing arts, Wolf Trap draws top music acts, dance and musical theater to its outdoor amphitheater. In the colder months, performers take the stage in the intimate Barns at Wolf Trap.
🔀 Off map at A1 ✉ 1645 Trap Road, Vienna, VA
☎ 703/255-1900 🚇 West Falls Church, then Wolf Trap express bus (every 20 min)

Restaurants

PRICES

Prices are approximate, based on a 3-course meal for one person.
$$$ over $50
$$ $30–$50
$ under $30

DR. GRANVILLE MOORE'S ($$)

www.granvillemoores.com
Formerly a doctor's office, Granville Moore's now soothes with Belgian beers and mussels. Nothing is ever reheated or frozen here.
⊞ M5 ⊠ 1238 H Street NE
☎ 202/399–2546 ⬤ Daily dinner (Fri, Sat until 3am) 🚇 Union Station, then taxi or bus X2

GRAPESEED ($$)

www.grapeseedbistro.com
"Choice" is the word at this bistro/wine bar, where scrumptious dishes and delectable wines are available in small portions for tasting.
⊞ Off map at A1 ⊠ 4865 Cordell Avenue, Bethesda, MD
☎ 301/986–9592
⬤ Mon–Fri lunch, dinner; Sat dinner only 🚇 Bethesda

INN AT 202 DOVER ($$)

The Inn's Peacock Restaurant and Lounge bills itself as Chesapeake Bay town's culinary hotspot. The menu offers classical and contemporary American cuisine, with the freshest of seafood.
⊞ Off map at M9 ⊠ 202 Dover Street, Eaton, MD
☎ 410/819–8007 ⬤ Thu–Mon dinner 🚇 Bethesda

INN AT LITTLE WASHINGTON ($$$)

www.theinnatlittle washington.com
An extravagant setting and an over-the-top American meal await the rich and famous who flock here to sample Chef Patrick O'Connell's kitchen. Two tables in the kitchen allow guests a piece of the action.
⊞ Off map at A9 ⊠ Main Street and Middle Street, Washington, VA
☎ 540/675–3800
⬤ Wed–Mon dinner

MAESTRO ($$$)

www.ritzcarlton.com
Located in the Ritz-Carlton, this restaurant's best tables are near the open kitchen, where Chef Fabio Trabocchi turns out overwhelming Italian menus.
⊞ Off map at A2 ⊠ 1700 Tyson's Boulevard, McLean, VA

PICNIC SPOTS

Washington, a city full of public spaces, offers many great spots for picnicking. Try the grassy expanses in Dupont Circle (▷ 87) or Rock Creek Park (▷ 86), on the Mall, around the Tidal Basin (▷ 37), and at Mount Vernon (▷ 103). Short on supplies? Try Marvelous Market (▷ 94) or Dean and Deluca (▷ 80).

☎ 703/506–4300
⬤ Mon–Sat dinner; Sun brunch

PHO 75 ($)

Pho, a Vietnamese noodle dish often eaten at breakfast in Vietnam, is served here in nearly 20 varieties—all of them tasty. Spoons are provided if you're not adept with chopsticks.
⊞ A6 ⊠ 1721 Wilson Boulevard, Arlington, VA
☎ 703/525–7355 ⬤ Daily 9–8 🚇 Rosslyn

RAY'S THE STEAKS ($$)

This stripped-down and reasonably priced bistro focuses on serving some of the best steaks in town. No reservations taken.
⊞ A6 ⊠ 2300 Wilson Boulevard, Arlington, VA
☎ 703/841–7297 ⬤ Daily dinner 🚇 Courthouse

RESTAURANT EVE ($$$)

www.restauranteve.com
The decor at Cathal Armstrong's restaurant, in an "Eden" theme, sets the stage for what comes next, Modern American cuisine that's truly inspired. Take your pick of several courses from the tasting menus.
⊞ Off map at E9
⊠ 110 South Pitt Street, Alexandria, VA
☎ 703/706–0450
⬤ Bistro: Mon–Fri lunch, dinner; Sat dinner. Tasting Room: Mon–Sat dinner

Washington DC has a range of accommodation options, from bed-and-breakfasts and boutique guesthouses to chain and business-class hotels.

Introduction

Forced to cater to all, from lobbyists oozing money to those in town for the free museums, from bigwigs seeking attention to those flying under the radar—intentionally or not—Washington's rooms suit everyone.

Diplomats at Breakfast
The high-end and business-class hotels tend to be near the halls of power, whether in Georgetown rowhouses, at the White House or on Capitol Hill. Downtown, also has its fair share. There's a good chance that if you stay in one of the pricier digs you'll run into diplomats at breakfast and brush shoulders with heads of state (or their security guards) in the elevator.

A Slower Pace
DC's boutique hotels and cool guesthouses are in the shadier areas of Northwest DC. Guests in these areas will enjoy a slightly slower pace and smaller crowds, and the commute to the Mall and Hill is negligible.

Off season? Not in DC
Summers bring tourists and winters bring policy makers and lobbyists. In fact, when Congress is in session, it's often more expensive to get a room during the week than on the weekend. Your best bet is to head for the suburbs, often as exciting as the District.

WHERE THE PRESIDENTS LIVE

In the White House, correct? Not when it's being renovated. George Washington lived in New York and Philadelphia, before the Capitol moved to DC. James Madison lived in the Octagon House (18th Street NW and New York Avenue) after the British burned the White House to the ground. Calvin Coolidge hosted Charles Lindbergh at the Patterson House (15 Dupont Circle) while the White House was being renovated. Harry S. Truman moved out for renovations also—to the nearby Blair House at 1651 Pennsylvania Avenue, where two Puerto Rican nationalists tried to assassinate him.

Budget Hotels

PRICES

Expect to pay up to $175 for a double room in a budget hotel.

ADAMS INN
www.adamsinn.com
This Victorian bed-and-breakfast encompasses three houses on a quiet street near the bustling strip of Adams-Morgan. 26 rooms.
✚ F1 ✉ 1746 Lanier Place NW ☎ 800/578–6807, fax 202/319–7958 Ⓜ Woodley Park–Zoo, then 10-min walk

BETHESDA COURT HOTEL
www.bethesdacourtwashdc.com
This three-story inn with an English courtyard serves complimentary afternoon tea. 74 rooms.
✚ Off map at A1 ✉ 7740 Wisconsin Avenue, Bethesda, MD ☎ 301/656–2100 Ⓜ Friendship Heights

CHURCHILL HOTEL
www.thechurchillhotel.com
The Beaux Arts Churchill provides large, comfortable rooms, a helpful staff, and a hilltop view over Dupont Circle.
✚ E3 ✉ 1914 Connecticut Avenue NW ☎ 202/ 7097–2000 or 800/424–2464 reservations Ⓜ Dupont Circle

HOSTELLING INTERNATIONAL WASHINGTON, DC
www.hiwashingtondc.org
Families may be able to get a room together in this well-kept hostel with bunk-beds, if it isn't busy.
✚ G5 ✉ 1009 11th Street NW ☎ 202/737–2333, fax 202/737–1508 Ⓜ McPherson Square, Metro Center

HOTEL HARRINGTON
www.hotel-harrington.com
This is your basic clean, no-frills hotel, but with a great location. The Mall and many museums are just a few blocks away. 245 rooms.
✚ G6 ✉ 436 11th Street NW ☎ 202/628–8140 or 800/424–8532, fax 202/347–3924 Ⓜ Metro Center

HOTEL MADERA
www.hotelmadera.com
A hip boutique hotel attached to a cool restaurant, Madera sports large rooms in bold tones. Service is excellent; you can even keep a "stow-away bag" of personal belongings here for your next trip.
✚ E4 ✉ 1310 New Hampshire Avenue ☎ 202/296–7600, fax 202/293–2476 Ⓜ Dupont Circle

BED-AND-BREAKFAST

To find reasonably priced accommodations in small guesthouses and private homes, contact the following bed-and-breakfast service: Bed 'n' Breakfast Accommodations Ltd. of Washington, DC (✉ Box 12011, Washington DC, 20005 ☎ 877/893–3233).

HOTEL TABARD INN
www.tabardinn.com
This charming old inn with plush antique rooms also sports a cozy lounge with a fireplace and a top-notch restaurant.
✚ F4 ✉ 1739 N Street NW ☎ 202/785–1277, fax 202/785–6173 Ⓜ Dupont Circle

KALORAMA GUEST HOUSE
www.kaloramaguesthouse.com
These Victorian town houses filled with 19th-century furnishings are near the Zoo and Adams-Morgan.
✚ E2 ✉ 1854 Mintwood Place NW ☎ 800/974–6750, fax 202/ 319–1262 Ⓜ Woodley Park–Zoo
✚ D1 ✉ 2700 Cathedral Avenue NW ☎ 202/328–0860 or 800/974–9101, fax 202/328–8730 Ⓜ Woodley Park–Zoo

WOODLEY PARK GUEST HOUSE
www.dcinns.com
An intimate bed-and-breakfast near the Zoo, this guesthouse offers individualized rooms filled with antiques. They are "not able to accommo-date young children." 18 rooms.
✚ D1 ✉ 2647 Woodley Road NW ☎ 866/667–0218 Ⓜ Woodley Park–Zoo

Mid-Range Hotels

AKWAABA DC

www.akwaaba.com
A literary-themed luxurious bed and breakfast owned by the former editor of *Essence*, Akwaaba sits in a well-located town house.
✚ F3 ✉ 1708 16th Street NW ☎ 877/899–3233, fax 718/455–9697 🚇 Dupont Circle

BEACON HOTEL

www.capitalhotelswdc.com
With a popular bar and grill, this lively hotel has well-sized rooms and a steady clientele of business travelers.
✚ F4 ✉ 1615 Rhode Island Avenue NW ☎ 800/821–4367 or 202/296–2100, fax 202/331–0227 🚇 Dupont Circle

CAPITOL HILL SUITES

www.capitolhillsuites.com
Within steps of the Library of Congress and the Capitol, this collection of tidy suites is home to several members of Congress.
✚ K7 ✉ 200 C Street SE ☎ 202/543–6000, fax 202/547–2608 🚇 Capitol South

EMBASSY SUITES

Aside from a magnificent eight-story lush atrium, visitors here enjoy large two-room suites, complimentary breakfast and a free nightly reception.
✚ E4 ✉ 1250 22nd Street NW ☎ 202/857–3388, fax 202/293–3173 🚇 Foggy Bottom

THE FAIRFAX AT EMBASSY ROW

www.starwoodhotels.com/westin
On one of Washington's loveliest streets, this former home of Al Gore feels like an old-boys club dressed in late 19th-century furniture.
✚ E3 ✉ 2100 Massachusetts Avenue NW ☎ 202/293–2100, fax 202/293–0641 🚇 Dupont Circle

FOUR POINTS SHERATON

www.starwoodhotels.com/fourpoints
This newly renovated and well-located hotel offers a long list of amenities and

the Disrict Grill Restaurant and Bar.
✚ G5 ✉ 1201 K Street NW ☎ 888/481–7192 or 202/289–7600, fax 202/349–2215 🚇 Metro Center

HENLEY PARK HOTEL

www.henleypark.com
A bit of Britain in a developing neighborhood, this Tudor-style hotel is part of the National Historic Trust. 96 rooms.
✚ H5 ✉ 926 Massachusetts Avenue NW ☎ 800/222–8474, fax 202/638–6740 🚇 Mount Vernon Square, Gallery Place or Metro Center

HOTEL MONTICELLO

www.monticellohotel.com
This homey hotel offers 47 apartments off a side-street in Georgetown. It has been recently revamped and retains its high regard for customer service.
✚ D4 ✉ 1075 Thomas Jefferson Street NW ☎ 202/337–0900 or 800/388–2410, fax 202/333–6526 🚇 Foggy Bottom

HOTEL PALOMAR

www.hotelpalomar-dc.com
This arts-themed Kimpton hotel takes advantage of nearby galleries by hosting artists and curators at evening discussions over wine. The rooms are large and amenities abound. 335 rooms.
✚ E4 ✉ 2121 P Street NW ☎ 877/866–3070, fax 202/448–1801 🚇 Dupont Circle

HOTEL ROUGE
www.rougehotel.com
Decked out in rich reds and contrasting pale colors, Rouge is distinctly hip and urban. Bar Rouge downstairs draws the same jet set.
✚ F4 ✉ 1315 16th Street NW
☎ 202/232–8000 or 800/738–1202,
fax 202/667–9827
Ⓜ Dupont Circle

JURYS NORMANDY INN
http://washingtondchotels.jurydoyle.com
This European-style hotel, on a quiet embassy-lined street is popular among diplomats. There is a wine and cheese reception every Tuesday evening. Use of a health club at a sister hotel nearby. 75 rooms.
✚ E2 ✉ 2118 Wyoming Avenue NW
☎ 202/483–1350,
fax 202/387–8241
Ⓜ Dupont Circle

LATHAM HOTEL
www.thelatham.com
This small, 143-room colonial-style hotel on one of Georgetown's main streets offers views of busy M Street and the C&O Canal. The hotel features Michel Richard Citronelle (▷ 80), one of Washington's best restaurants. There's the added bonus of a rooftop pool.
✚ D4 ✉ 3000 M Street NW
☎ 202/726–5000, fax 202/337–4250 Ⓜ Foggy Bottom

MARRIOTT WARDMAN PARK
www.marriott.com/WASDT
The huge, brick Victorian hotel looms over the Woodley Park Metro stop, consequently offering a nice view of Rock Creek Park. Amenities abound. 1,340 rooms.
✚ D1 ✉ 2660 Woodley Road NW ☎ 202/328–2000, fax 202/234–0015 Ⓜ Woodley Park–Zoo

MORRISON-CLARK INN HOTEL
www.morrisonclark.com
Created by merging two 1864 town houses, this 54-room inn, part of the National Historic Trust, has individually decorated, colonial rooms.
✚ G4 ✉ 1015 L Street NW
☎ 202/898–1200 or 800/332–7898,
fax 202/289–8576
Ⓜ Mount Vernon Square

THE QUINCY
www.thequincy.com
These well-located suites

offer quick access to the White House, Dupont Circle and Downtown.
✚ F4 ✉ 1823 L Street NW
☎ 202/223–4320 or 800/424–2970 Ⓜ Farragut North

RIVER INN
www.theriverinn.com
This small, all-suite hotel is near Georgetown, George Washington University and the John F. Kennedy Center. Rooms are homey if modest. 126 rooms.
✚ D5 ✉ 924 25th Street NW ☎ 888/874–0100,
fax 202/337–6520
Ⓜ Foggy Bottom

SWANN HOUSE
www.swannhouse.com
Converted from an 1883 Dupont Circle mansion, this bed-and-breakfast wows with feather beds, chandeliers and original molding.
✚ F3 ✉ 1808 New Hampshire Avenue NW
☎ 202/265–4414,
fax 202/265–6755
Ⓜ Dupont Circle

TOPAZ HOTEL
www.topazhotel.com
Bright earthy stripes and polka dots grace the walls and fabrics here at this "wellness"-theme hotel, which serves energy shakes in the morning. The large rooms contain a desk, settee and dressing room.
✚ F4 ✉ 1733 N Street NW
☎ 202/393–3000 or 800/775–1202, fax 202/785–9581
Ⓜ Dupont Circle

Luxury Hotels

FOUR SEASONS HOTEL

www.fourseasons.com/washington

A gathering place for Washington's elite, this hotel, redesigned by Pierre Yves Rochon, features rooms with custom-made furniture and stunning artwork. 211 rooms.

D4 ⊠ 2800 Pennsylvania Avenue NW ☎ 202/342–0444 or 800/819–5053, fax 202/944–2076 🚇 Foggy Bottom

HAY-ADAMS HOTEL

www.hayadams.com

Looking like a mansion on the outside and an English country house within, this hotel has a picture-postcard White House view—ask for a room on the south side. 145 rooms.

F5 ⊠ 800 16th Street NW ☎ 202/638–6600 or 800/853–6807, fax 202/638–2716 🚇 McPherson Square

HOTEL MONACO

www.monaco-dc.com

Built in 1839 by the designer of the Washing-ton Monument, Monaco sports rooms with vaulted ceilings and timeless furnishings around a landscaped courtyard.

H5 ⊠ 700 F Street NW ☎ 800/649–1202, fax 202/628–7277 🚇 Gallery Place–Chinatown

MANDARIN ORIENTAL

www.mandarinoriental.com/washington

This large modern hotel, a short walk from the Tidal Basin, sports subdued rooms with "Asian" flare. The restaurants, CityZen (▷ 52) and Empress Lounge are popular. 400 rooms.

H7 ⊠ 1330 Maryland Avenue SW ☎ 202/554–8588 or 888/888–1778, fax 202/554–8999 🚇 Smithsonian

MANSION ON O STREET

www.omansion.com

Popular among the jet set, this set of Victorian town houses offers luxurious and creatively themed rooms.

E4 ⊠ 2020 O Street NW ☎ 202/496–2000, fax 202/833–8333 🚇 Dupont Circle

RENAISSANCE MAYFLOWER

The ornate lobby of this grand hotel glistens with gilded trim. The rooms were once home to FDR.

F4 ⊠ 1127 Connecticut Avenue NW ☎ 202/347–3000 or 800/228–7697, fax 202/776–9182 🚇 Farragut North

RITZ-CARLTON, GEORGETOWN

www.ritzcarlton.com/georgetown

Housed in the former Georgetown incinerator, this sleek hotel is luxurious and cozy.

C4 ⊠ 3100 South Street NW ☎ 202/912–4100, fax 202/912–4199 🚇 Foggy Bottom

SOFITEL, LAFAYETTE SQUARE

www.sofitel.com

This Jazz-Age hotel caters to an international clientele. Enjoy the chic rooms and world-class food at Café 15. 237 rooms.

G5 ⊠ 806 15th Street NW ☎ 202/730–8800, fax 202/730–8500 🚇 McPherson Square

WILLARD INTERCONTINENTAL

www.washington.intercontinental.com

Heads of state have made the Willard home since 1853. The lobby is Beaux Arts. 341 rooms.

G5 ⊠ 1401 Pennsylvania Avenue NW ☎ 202/628–9100 or 888/424–6835, fax 202/637–7326 🚇 McPherson Square

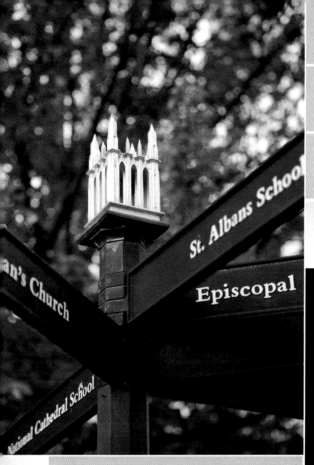

Need to Know

This section contains essential information about preparing for your journey to Washington, how to get around once you are there, and other practicalities.

Planning Ahead

When to Go

There is no bad time to visit Washington. Spring is busiest, when the city's cherry trees are in blossom. October and November bring brilliant foliage. Summer, although crowded and sweltering, sees a chockablock calendar of special events, many of which are free.

TIME

Washington is on Eastern Standard Time. Clocks go forward one hour in March and go back in late October.

AVERAGE DAILY MAXIMUM TEMPERATURES

JAN	FEB	MAR	APR	MAY	JUN	JUL	AUG	SEP	OCT	NOV	DEC
42°F	45°F	53°F	64°F	75°F	83°F	87°F	84°F	78°F	67°F	55°F	45°F
6°C	7°C	12°C	18°C	24°C	28°C	31°C	29°C	26°C	19°C	13°C	7°C

Spring (mid-March to May) is extremely pleasant, with flowers and trees in bloom throughout the city.

Summer (June to early September) is hot and humid, with temperatures sometimes reaching 95°F (35°C) or more.

Fall (mid-September to November) is comfortable, and sometimes bracing.

Winter (December to mid-March) varies from year to year: It can be extremely cold or surprisingly warm. The occasional snowfall shuts the city down.

WHAT'S ON

January Antiques Show (☎ 202/338 9560). Martin Luther King Jr. Birthday Observations. Restaurant Week (www.washington.org/ restaurantwk).

February President's Day (☎ 202/619–7275). Chinese New Year's Parade (☎ 202/638–1041).

March St. Patrick's Day Festival (☎ 202/637–2474). Organist's Bach Marathon (☎ 202/363–2202). Smithsonian Kite Flying Festival (☎ 202/357–2700).

April National Cherry Blossom Festival (☎ 877/44BLOOM). White House Spring Garden Tour (☎ 202/456–2200). Filmfest DC (www.film festdc.org).

May Washington National Cathedral Flower Mart (☎ 202/537–6200). Military Band Summer Concert Series (☎ 202/433–4011). Memorial Day Concert (☎ 202/972–9556).

June Capitol Pride Festival (☎ 202/797–3510).

July Smithsonian Folklife Festival (☎ 202/275–1150).

Independence Day (Jul 4, ☎ 202/619–7222).

September National Symphony Orchestra Labor Day Concert (☎ 202/467–4600). Adams-Morgan Day (☎ 202/232–1960).

October Marine Corps Marathon (☎ 800/786–8762). Taste of DC Festival (☎ 202/789–7000).

November Veterans' Day (☎ 703/607–8000).

December National Christmas Tree Lighting (☎ 202/208–1631).

Useful Websites

www.si.edu

The Smithsonian Institution site features a directory of its 19 museums, schedules of events and exhibits, information about research and publications and a link to the gift shop.

www.washington.org

This site is presented by the Washington DC, Convention and Tourism board. You can make hotel reservations, gather information about the different neighborhoods and find out about annual events.

www.culturaltourismdc.org

The website of this nonprofit coalition of DC cultural and neighborhood organizations hosts comprehensive and easy-to-navigate listings of DC districts, walks, events, and attractions that you might not be able to find elsewhere.

www.fly2dc.com

The online hub of Washington Flyer, the official magazine of the Metropolitan Washington Airports Authority, Fly2DC is a solid resource on flying in and out of DC.

www.opentable.com

Allows diners to check availability and make reservations at most Washington restaurants.

www.washingtonpost.com

The newspaper's site features a visitor's guide, including airport status reports, a calendar of events and reviews of nightlife and restaurants.

www.washingtoncitypaper.com

The site of this alternative weekly carries the newspaper's superb arts coverage as well as a "Restaurant Finder," with reviews from the paper's critics and visitors to the site.

www.senate.gov and www.house.gov

Congress website including information on upcoming votes, history and how to visit.

GOOD TRAVEL SITES

www.fodors.com

A complete travel-planning site. You can research prices and weather; book air tickets, cars and rooms; ask questions (and get answers) from fellow travelers; and find links to other sites.

www.wmata.com

The Washington Metropolitan Transit Authority site features maps of the Metro and bus systems, plus information on delays and vacation schedules.

INTERNET CAFÉS

Kramerbooks and Afterwords Café
(▷ 90)
🔲 F4 ✉ 1517 Connecticut Avenue NW, Dupont Circle
☎ 202/387-1400
🕐 Sun–Thu 7.30am–1am, Fri–Sat 24 hours 🖥 15 min of free e-mail at bar

Java House
🔲 F3 ✉ 1645 Q Street NW
☎ 202/387-6622 🕐 Daily 7am–10pm 🖥 Free WiFi (unlimited)

Getting There

BUS TRAVEL

Several luxury bus compa-
nies—some with free WiFi
and onboard movies—pick up
passengers throughout
Washington and offer inexpensive rides to New York.
Try www.dc2ny.com or
www.boltbus.com.

TRAIN TRAVEL

Amtrak trains leave on tracks
stretching out the back of
Union Station. Service to
New York takes 3–4 hours;
it's almost 8 hours to Boston.
The high-speed Acela cuts it
down to 3 hours and 6.5
hours respectively. Two
less-expensive commuter
lines service the Virginia
and Maryland suburbs on
weekdays.

AIRPORTS

Flying time to Washington, District of Columbia, is 1 hour
from New York, 5 hours 40 minutes from Los Angeles and
6 hours from London. The major airports include Ronald
Reagan National Airport, Dulles International Airport and
Baltimore-Washington International Airport (BWI).

FROM RONALD REAGAN NATIONAL AIRPORT

Ronald Reagan National Airport (☎ 703/417–
8000, www.mwaa.com/national) is in Virginia,
4 miles (6.4km) south of downtown and the
closest to central Washington. A taxi to downtown takes about 20 minutes and costs around
$10–$20. SuperShuttle (☎ 800/258–3826)
offers an airport-to-door service for $12 per
person 24 hours a day. The blue and yellow
Metro lines run from the airport to downtown,
with stations next to terminals B and C
(🅜 Mon–Thu 5am–midnight, Fri 5am–3am,
Sat 7am–3am, Sun 7am–midnight). Fare cards
($1.65) can be bought from machines on level
2 near the pedestrian bridges linking the two
terminals.
Metro information (☎ 202/637–7000).
Private Car (☎ 800/878–7743) will arrange for
a car or limousine to meet you at the airport.
Cost is around $49 for a sedan and $104 for a
limousine, plus an 18 percent tip.

FROM DULLES INTERNATIONAL AIRPORT

Dulles International Airport (☎ 703/572–2700,
www.mwaa.com/dulles) is 26 miles (42km) west

of Washington. A taxi to the city takes around 40 minutes and costs around $55. The Washington Flyer Coach (☎ 888/927–4359) goes from the airport to the West Falls Church Metro. Buses leave the airport every half hour Mon–Fri 5.45am–10.15pm, Sat–Sun 7.45am–10.15pm. The 25-minute trip costs $9 ($16 round-trip). SuperShuttle (☎ 800/258–3826) costs $27 per person, plus $8 for each additional person. Private Car (☎ 800/878–7743) costs around $81 for a sedan and $131 for a limousine, plus an 18 percent gratuity.

FROM BWI AIRPORT
Baltimore-Washington International Airport (☎ 800/435–9294, www.bwiairport.com) is in Maryland, 30 miles (48km) northeast of Washington. A taxi from the airport takes around 45 minutes and costs $60–$65. SuperShuttle (☎ 800/258–3826) costs $35, plus $12 for each additional person. Free shuttle buses run between airline terminals and the train station. Amtrak (☎ 800/872–7245) and MARC (☎ 800/325–7245) trains run between the airport and Union Station. The 40-minute ride costs $11–$38 (depending on day and time) on Amtrak and $6 on MARC (weekdays only). With Private Car you'll pay $95 for a sedan or $145 for a limousine, plus an 18 percent gratuity.

INSURANCE
Check your policy and buy any necessary supplements. It is vital that travel insurance covers medical expenses, in addition to accident, trip cancellation, baggage loss, and theft. Also make sure the policy covers any continuing treatment for a more chronic condition.

ENTRY REQUIREMENTS
For the latest passport and visa information, look up the embassy website at www.britainusa.com or www.usembassy.org.uk. The authorities are now subjecting more people to even more security checks. Leave plenty of time for clearing security, and be sure to check the latest advice.

AIRLINES
Major air carriers serving the three airports (Ronald Reagan National Airport, Dulles International Airport and Baltimore-Washington International Airport) include:

Air Canada	☎ 888/247–2262	**KLM Royal Dutch**	☎ 800/225–2525
Air France	☎ 800/321–4538	**Lufthansa**	☎ 800/645–3880
America West	☎ 800/235–9292	**Midwest Airlines**	☎ 800/452–2022
British Airways	☎ 800/247–9297	**Northwest**	☎ 800/225–2525
Continental	☎ 800/523–3273	**Saudi Arabian Airlines**	☎ 800/472–8342
Delta	☎ 800/221–1212	**United**	☎ 800/241–6522
El Al	☎ 800/223–6700	**US Airways**	☎ 800/428–4322
Icelandair	☎ 800/223–5500	**Virgin Atlantic**	☎ 800/862–8621
Japan Airlines	☎ 800/525–3663		

For less expensive flights, contact Southwest Airlines ☎ 800/435–9792, AirTran Airways ☎ 800/247–8726 or JetBlue Airways ☎ 800/538–2583

Getting Around

VISITORS WITH DISABILITIES

Museums and other public buildings are often equipped with ramps and elevators and are usually accessible to wheelchair users. Wheelchair access to Metro trains is via elevators from street level; details at www.wmata.com. Information on various DC locations can be found at www.disabilityguide.com.

METRO TRANSFERS

To transfer to a bus after leaving the Metro, get a transfer from the dispenser next to the escalator that goes down to the train level.

PUBLIC TRANSPORTATION

● The subway (Metro) and bus (Metrobus) systems are run by the Washington Metropolitan Area Transit Authority (WMATA).
● Maps of the Metro system and some bus schedules are available in all Metro stations or at WMATA headquarters ✉ 600 5th Street NW.
● For general information call ☎ 202/637–7000 🕓 Mon–Fri 6am–10.30pm, Sat–Sun 7am–10.30pm.
● Lost and Found ☎ 202/962–1195 Transit police ☎ 202/962–2121

BUSES

● Bus signs are blue and red and white.
● The bus system covers a much wider area than the Metro. The fare within the city is $1.35.
● Free bus-to-bus transfers are available from the driver and are good for about 2 hours at designated Metrobus transfer points.

METRO

● The city's subway system, the Metro, is one of the cleanest and safest in the country. You need a farecard to ride, both to enter and exit the train area. Farecard machines, located in the stations, take coins and $1, $5, $10 and $20 notes. The most change the machine will give you is about $5, so don't use a large bill if you are buying a low-value card.
● Metro stations are marked by tall brown pillars with a large, white "M" at the top. A colored stripe under the "M" indicates the line or lines that are serviced by the station.
● Trains run every few minutes 🕓 Mon–Thu 5am–midnight; Fri 5am–3am; Sat 7am–3am; Sun 7am–midnight.
● The basic peak fare ($1.65) increases based on the length of your trip. It is cheaper at off peak times. Maps in stations tell you both the rush-hour fare and regular fare to any destination station.
● Insert your farecard into the slot on the front of the turnstile. Retrieve it once the gate opens as you will need it to exit. On exiting, insert the

farecard into the turnstile. If your card contains the exact fare you will not get it back; if your card still has some money on it, it will pop out the top of the turnstile. A red "STOP" light means you need more money on your card to leave the station and must go to the "Add fare" machine; insert your card and the machine will tell you how much additional fare is owed; pay that fare and return to the exit turnstile.

● The farecards are reusable until the card has a value of less than $1.65. Then, should you need another farecard, your old card can be used as cash in the farecard machine by putting it in the "Used Farecard Trade-In" slot.

● A $7.80 one-day pass is available for unlimited trips on weekends, holidays or after 9.30am weekdays. Passes are available online and at every Metro station.

● Transfer to a bus upon leaving the Metro. The ability to trasfer to a bus from the Metro is only available if you have a SmartTrip card.

TAXIS

● Taxis are abundant and safe in Washington. Look for cars with white lights on their roof tops, which signals they are open. Fares are $3 upon entering the cab and 25 cents for each additional one sixth of a mile. Other charges that may be added: Luggage $2 a piece; if you're coming from the airport, there's an additional charge of $4; each additional passenger is $1.50. No taxi trip within the District of Columbia can exceed $19.

DRIVING

● Driving in Washington is for the patient only.

● Although "right turn on red" is permitted, most downtown intersections have signs forbidding it from 7am–7pm, or banning it outright. Virginia also allows "left turn on red" when turning into a one-way street from another one-way street.

● The speed limit in the city is 25mph (40kph), unless otherwise stated.

● Seat belts are mandatory for the driver and front-seat passenger.

CAR RENTAL

Alamo ☎ 800/462–5266
Avis ☎ 800/331–1212
Budget ☎ 800/527–0700
Dollar ☎ 800/800–4000
Hertz ☎ 800/654–3131
National ☎ 800/227–7368

You will have to provide a credit card and drivers under 25 years old may have to pay a local surcharge to the rental company.

PARKING IN DC

Parking is a problem in Washington, as the public parking areas fill up quickly with local workers' cars; you might prefer to use public transportation. If you park on city streets, check the signs to make sure it is permitted: Green and white signs show when parking is allowed, red and white signs when it is not. Parking on most main streets is not permitted during rush hours, and if you park illegally your car is likely to get towed. If it does, call ☎ 202/727–5000 to find out where it is and how to get it back. If it is towed on a weekend (after 7pm Friday) you'll have to wait until Monday to retrieve it.

Essential Facts

MONEY

The unit of currency is the dollar (= 100 cents). Notes (bills) come in denominations of $1, $5, $10, $20, $50 and $100; coins come in 25¢ (a quarter), 10¢ (a dime), 5¢ (a nickel) and 1¢ (a penny). Sales tax in Washington, DC, is 5.75 percent, hotel tax 14.5 percent (9.75 percent in Virginia) and food and beverage tax 10 percent.

5 dollars

10 dollars

50 dollars

100 dollars

CUSTOMS

● Visitors aged 21 or more may import duty free: 200 cigarettes or 50 cigars or 2kg of tobacco; 1 litre (1 US quart) of alcohol; and gifts up to $100 in value.

● Restricted import items include meat, seeds, plants and fruit.

● Some medication bought over the counter abroad may be prescription-only in the US and may be confiscated. Bring a doctor's certificate for essential medication.

ELECTRICITY

● The electricity supply is 110 volts AC, and plugs are standard two pins. Foreign visitors will need an adaptor and voltage converter for their own appliances.

EMBASSIES AND CONSULATES

● Canada ⊠ 501 Pennsylvania Avenue NW ☎ 202/682–1740, www.canadainternational. gc.ca/washington

● Ireland ⊠ 2234 Massachusetts Avenue NW ☎ 202/462–3939, www.irelandemb.org

● United Kingdom ⊠ 3100 Massachusetts Avenue NW ☎ 202/588–6500, www.britainusa.com

EMERGENCY PHONE NUMBERS

Police 911
Fire 911
Ambulance 911
● For all other non-urgent matters 311

LOST PROPERTY

● Metro or Metrobus ☎ 202/962–1195
● Smithsonian museums ☎ 202/633–1000
● Other lost articles, check with the city at ☎ 311

MAIL

● The North Capitol Station has the longest hours ⊠ 2 Massachusetts Avenue NE ☎ 202/523–2928 🕙 Mon–Fri 9–7, Sat–Sun 9–5.

● Other branches: Farragut ✉ 1800 M Street NW ☎ 202/833–9615 ⏰ Mon–Fri 9–5; L'Enfant Plaza ✉ 437 L'Enfant Plaza SW ☎ 202/863–1291 ⏰ Mon–Fri 8–5; Washington Square ✉ 1050 Connecticut Avenue NW ☎ 202/728–0349 ⏰ Mon–Fri 9–5; Union Station ✉ 50 Massachsetts Avenue NE ☎ 202/523–2057 ⏰ Mon–Fri 7–5, Sat 7–3.30

MONEY MATTERS
● Tipping is expected for all services. As a guide the following applies:
Restaurants 20 percent–15 percent
Hairdressers 15 percent
Taxis 15 percent
Chambermaids $1 per day
Porters $1 per bag

NEWSPAPERS AND MAGAZINES
● Washington has two major daily newspapers, *The Washington Post* and *The Washington Times,* which is more conservative.
● The *City Paper*, a free weekly with an emphasis on entertainment, is available from newspaper boxes around town and at many restaurants, clubs and other outlets; (www.washingtoncitypaper.com).
● In addition, various neighborhood weekly newspapers serve Capitol Hill, Georgetown, Adams-Morgan and other areas.
● *Washingtonian*, a monthly magazine, has a calendar of events, dining information and articles about the city and its prominent people.
● *Where/Washington*, a monthly magazine listing popular things to do, is free at most hotels.
● Other national newspapers are available.

OPENING HOURS
● Stores ⏰ Generally Mon–Sat 10–6; Sun 12–5
● Banks ⏰ Mon–Fri 9–3, although hours can vary
● Post offices ⏰ Mon–Fri 8-5; some offices open Sat

STREET NAMES
Washington's street names are based on a quadrant system, the center of which is the Capitol building. Numbered streets run north–south, while lettered streets run east–west. Both progress with distance from the Capitol. There is no "J" Street, eliminated to prevent confusion with "I" Street. For example, 1900 R Street NW is 19 blocks west and 17 blocks north of the Capitol, as "R" is the 17th letter if you skip "J." Diagonal avenues cut across the grid. They are named after the States based on their date of statehood and their proximity to the Capitol. Delaware, the "First State" is closest.

SMOKING
DC, once thought a safe haven for smokers, is becoming less and less friendly to those who want to light up. Smoking is banned in almost all indoor public places, including restautants, bars and clubs.

TOILETS
It's best to use those in large hotels and stores, galleries and museums.

RADIO

- FM Radio 88.5 (WAMU)– National Public Radio (news)
- 90.9 (WETA)–Classical
- 98.7 (WMZQ)–Country
- 99.5 (WIHT)–Pop
- 101.1 (WWDC)–Rock
- 107.3 (WRQX)–Adult Contemporary

LOCAL BLOGS

- www.metrocurean.com– local restaurant news and reviews.
- www.dcist.com–thorough news and goings-on site.
- http://blog.washington post.com/goingoutgurus– postings by the Washington Post's team of "Going out Gurus."

PUBLIC HOLIDAYS

- Jan 1: New Year's Day
- Third Mon in Jan: Birthday of Martin Luther King Jr.
- Third Mon in Feb: Presidents' Day
- Last Mon in May: Memorial Day
- Jul 4: Independence Day
- First Mon in Sep: Labor Day
- Second Mon in Oct: Columbus Day
- Nov 11: Veterans Day
- Fourth Thu in Nov: Thanksgiving Day
- Dec 25: Christmas Day
- On public holidays banks and post offices close, stores and restaurants stay open.

STATE REGULATIONS

- You must be 21 years old to drink alcohol in Washington, and you may be required to produce proof of age and photo ID.

STUDENTS

- Holders of an International Student Identity Card may be entitled to discounts.

VISITOR INFORMATION

- Washington, DC, Convention and Tourism Corporation ⊠ 901 7th Street NW, 4th Floor, Washington, DC, 20001 ☎ 202/789–7000, fax 202/789–7037, www.washington.org The Visitor Center is at ⊠ 1300 Pennsylvania Avenue NW, in the Ronald Reagan Building ☎ 866/324–7386, www.downtowndc.org ◐ Mon–Sat 9am–5pm
- National Park Service ⊠ 1849 C Street NW,

MEDICAL TREATMENT

- The hospital closest to downtown is George Washington University Hospital ⊠ 900 23rd Street NW ☎ 202/715-4000, urgent care visits to Washington DC hotels ☎ 202/216–9100
- 1–800–DOCTORS ☎ 800/362-8677 is a referral service that locates doctors, dentists and urgent care clinics in the greater Washington area.
- The DC Dental Society operates a referral line ☎ 202/547–7613, www.dcdental.org ◐ Mon–Fri 8–4.
- CVS operates 24-hour pharmacies ⊠ 2240 M Street NW ☎ 202/296–9877; ⊠ 6514 Georgia Avenue ☎ 202/829–5234; ⊠ 6 Dupont Circle NW ☎ 202/785–1466.

Washington DC 20240 ☎ 202/208–3818,
www.nps.gov

● The White House Visitor Center ✉ Baldridge
Hall in the Department of Commerce Building,
1450 Pennsylvania Avenue NW ☎ 202/208–
1631 ⏰ Daily 7.30–4

● National Park Service information kiosks can
be found on the Mall, near the White House,
next to the Vietnam Veterans Memorial and at
several other locations throughout the city.

● Dial-A-Park is a recording of events at Park
Service attractions in and around Washington
☎ 202/619–7275.

● Dial-A-Museum is a recording of exhibits and
special offerings at Smithsonian Institution
museums ☎ 202/633–1000.

WASHINGTON SLANG

● "Hill staffers"—staff for individual members of
Congress who work on Capitol Hill. Dominant
demographic in DC.

● "Inside the Beltway"—the "Beltway" is I–495,
which forms a circle around the District.
Generally refers to the American political
system and its insularity.

● "Foggy Bottom," "Langley"—agencies are
often referred to by their location. These are the
State Department and CIA, respectively.

● "NoVa"—short for "Northern Virginia," this
typically refers to Arlington and Alexandria.
Occasionally used as a term of derision.

TELEPHONES

To call Washington from the
UK, dial 00 1, Washington's
area code (202), and then
the number.
To call the UK from
Washington, dial 011 44, then
omit the first zero from the
area code.

SAFETY

Washington is as safe as any
large city. However, in part
because of the wide income
divide, crime statistics vary
hugely from block to block.
And tourist areas that are
safe during the day may not
be safe at night. At night
walk with someone rather
than alone; use taxis in less
populous areas.

PLACES OF WORSHIP

Episcopal: Washington National Cathedral	✉ Wisconsin and Massachusetts avenues NW ☎ 202/537–6200
Jewish: Adas Israel	✉ Connecticut Avenue and Porter Street NW ☎ 202/362–4433 🚇 Cleveland Park
Muslim: Islamic Mosque and Cultural Center	✉ 2551 Massachusetts Avenue NW ☎ 202/332–8343
Roman Catholic	National Shrine of the Immaculate Conception ✉ 400 Michigan Avenue NE ☎ 202/526–8300; Franciscan Monastery ✉ 1400 Quincy Street NE ☎ 202/526–6800

Timeline

EARLY DAYS

In 1770, President George Washington was authorized by Congress to build a Federal City. The following year, he hired Pierre Charles L'Enfant to design a city beside the Potomac River. According to legend, he sited the US Capitol in the exact middle of the 13 original states. By 1800, President Adams was able to occupy the unfinished White House, and Congress met in the Capitol, also unfinished. The population was by then around 3,000.

DOWN THE WIRE

In 1844, Samuel F. B. Morse transmitted the first telegraph message from the Capitol to Baltimore, Maryland.

1812 US declares war on Britain in response to the impressment of sailors from American ships and border disputes in Canada.

1814 The British sack Washington, burning the White House and the Capitol. The war ends with the Treaty of Ghent, ratified in late 1814.

1846 Congress accepts James Smithson's bequest and establishes the Smithsonian Institution.

1850 The slave trade is abolished in the District of Columbia.

1863 President Abraham Lincoln's Emancipation Proclamation frees the nation's slaves; many move to Washington.

1865 Lincoln is assassinated during a performance at Ford's Theatre.

1867 Howard University is chartered by Congress to educate blacks.

1876 The nation's centennial is celebrated with a fair in Philadelphia.

1901 The McMillan Commission oversees the city's beautification.

1907 Trains run to the new Union Station.

1922 The Lincoln Memorial is completed, 57 years after Lincoln's death.

1943 The Jefferson Memorial and Pentagon are completed.

1961 President John F. Kennedy plans the renovation of Pennsylvania Avenue. Residents are given the right to vote in presidential elections.

1968–73 Demonstrations against the Vietnam War are held on the National Mall.

1974 The Watergate Hotel becomes infamous as the site of the bungled Republican robbery attempt on Democratic headquarters. President Richard Nixon resigns as a result of the ensuing cover-up.

1976 The Metrorail opens.

1981 President Ronald Reagan is shot outside the Washington Hilton.

1991 Mayor Sharon Pratt Dixon Kelly becomes the first African American to lead a major US city.

2001 Terrorists highjack a passenger plane from Dulles Airport on September 11 and crash it into the Pentagon, killing 254 people.

2002 Two snipers terrorize the DC area for three weeks; there are 13 casualties.

2009 Barack Obama, the first African-American president in the nation's history, is inauguerated.

"I HAVE A DREAM"

On August 28, 1963, Martin Luther King Jr. delivered his vision of racial harmony from the steps of the Lincoln Memorial to a crowd of 200,000. Born in 1929, King had entered the ministry in 1955. As pastor of the Dexter Avenue Baptist Church in Montgomery, Alabama, he became the figurehead of the organized nonviolent civil-rights protests to end discrimination laws. His "I Have a Dream" speech ended a march on Washington by blacks and whites calling for reform. King was awarded the Nobel Peace Prize in 1964. His last sermon was at Washington National Cathedral in 1968—he was shot five days later in Memphis.

Below from left to right: Martin Luther King Jr.; Smithsonian Institute; Union Station; Vietnam Memorial; George Washington

Index

CITYPACK TOP 25
Washington

WRITTEN BY Mary Case and Bruce Walker
ADDITIONAL WRITING Matthew Cordell
UPDATED BY Heather Maher
COVER DESIGN AND DESIGN WORK Jacqueline Bailey
INDEXER Marie Lorimer
IMAGE RETOUCHING AND REPRO Sarah Montgomery and James Tims
PROJECT EDITOR Apostrophe S Limited
SERIES EDITOR Marie-Claire Jefferies

© **AA MEDIA LIMITED 2011**

First published 1997
New edition 2007
Reprinted Sep 2007
Information updated and verified for 2011

Colour separation by AA Digital Department
Printed and bound by Leo Paper Products, China

A CIP catalogue record for this book is available from the British Library.

ISBN 978-0-7495-5093-6

Published by AA Publishing, a trading name of AA Media Limited, whose registered office is Fanum House, Basing View, Basingstoke, Hampshire RG21 4EA. Registered number 06112600.

A04202
Maps in this title produced from mapping © MAIRDUMONT / Falk Verlag 2011
Transport map © Communicarta Ltd, UK

The Automobile Association would like to thank the following photographers, companies and picture libraries for their assistance in the preparation of this book.

Abbreviations for the picture credits are as follows: (t) top; (b) bottom; (l) left; (r) right; (AA) AA World Travel Library

F/C AA/Clive Sawyer; **B/Ca** AA/Clive Sawyer; **B/Cb** AA/Clive Sawyer; **B/Cc** AA/Ethel Davies; **B/Cd** Ethel Davies; **1** AA/Clive Sawyer; **2** AA/Clive Sawyer; **3** AA/Clive Sawyer; **4t** AA/Clive Sawyer; **4l** AA/Clive Sawyer; **5t** AA/Clive Sawyer; **5c** AA/Clive Sawyer; **6t** AA/Clive Sawyer; **6cl** AA/Clive Sawyer; **6c** AA/Ethel Davies; **6cr** AA/Clive Sawyer; **6bl** AA/Clive Sawyer; **6bc** AA/Clive Sawyer; **6br** AA/Ethel Davies; **7t** AA/Clive Sawyer; **7cl** AA/Clive Sawyer; **7c** AA/Ethel Davies; **7cr** AA/Clive Sawyer; **7bl** AA/Ethel Davies; **7bc** AA/Ethel Davies; **7br** AA/Clive Sawyer; **8** AA/Clive Sawyer; **9** AA/Clive Sawyer; **10t** AA/Clive Sawyer; **10tr** AA/Clive Sawyer; **10ct** AA/Clive Sawyer; **10cb** AA/Clive Sawyer; **10b** AA/Ethel Davies; **11tl** AA/Clive Sawyer; **11ct** AA/Max Jourdan; **11cb** AA/Harold Harris; **11b** AA/Clive Sawyer; **12** AA/Clive Sawyer; **13t** AA/Clive Sawyer; **13tl** Brand X Pictures; **13ct** AA/Clive Sawyer; **13c** Digital Vision; **13cb** Digital Vision; **13b** AA/Julian Love; **14t** AA/Clive Sawyer; **14tr** AA/Clive Sawyer; **14ct** AA//Julian Love; **14cb** Imagestate; **14b** AA/Julian Love; **15** AA/Clive Sawyer; **16t** AA/Julian Love; **16tr** AA/Clive Sawyer; **16cr** AA/Julian Love; **16br** AA/Julian Love; **17t** AA/Clive Sawyer; **17tl** Image 100; **17ctl** AA/Julian Love; **17cbl** AA/Julian Love; **17b** Stockbyte; **18t** AA/Julian Love; **18tr** AA/Clive Sawyer; **18ctr** AA/Julian Love; **18cbr** AA/Julian Love; **18br** AA/Julian Love; **19t** AA/Clive Sawyer; **19ct** AA/Clive Sawyer; **19c** AA/Ethel Davies; **19cbt** AA/Clive Sawyer; **19cb** Rock Creek Park; **19b** AA/Jim Holmes; **20/21** AA/Clive Sawyer; **24l** AA/Clive Sawyer; **24r** AA/Ethel Davies; **25** AA/Ethel Davies; **26t** AA/Clive Sawyer; **26b** AA/Julian Love; **27t** AA/Clive Sawyer; **27b** Courtesy of the International Spy Museum; **28** AA/Clive Sawyer; **29** AA/Harold Harris; **30** Photodisc; **31** AA/James Tims; **32** Bananastock; **33** AA/Clive Sawyer; **36** AA/Ethel Davies; **37l** © Dennis MacDonald/Alamy; **37r** AA/Ethel Davies; **38** AA/Julian Love; **39l** AA/Clive Sawyer; **39c** AA/Clive Sawyer; **39r** AA/Clive Sawyer; **40/41** AA/Julian Love; **41** AA/Julian Love; **42** AA/Ethel Davies; **43l** AA/Julian Love; **43r** AA/Julian Love; **44l** AA/Julian Love; **44c** AA/Julian Love; **44r** AA/Julian Love; **45rl** AA/Julian Love; **45c** AA/Julian Love; **45l** AA/Julian Love **46l** AA/Clive Sawyer; **46/47** AA/Clive Sawyer; **46r** AA/Clive Sawyer; **47l** AA/Ethel Davies; **47r** AA/Clive Sawyer; **48l** AA/Clive Sawyer; **48r** AA/Clive Sawyer; **49t** AA/Clive Sawyer; **49b** AA/Clive Sawyer; **50t** AA/Clive Sawyer; **50bl** AA/Ethel Davies; **50br** AA/Ethel Davies; **51** AA/Clive Sawyer; **52t** Digital Vision; **52c** AA/Douglas Corrance; **53** AA/Clive Sawyer; **56** AA/Clive Sawyer; **57l** AA/Ethel Davies; **57r** AA/Clive Sawyer; **58** AA/Ethel Davies; **58/59** AA/Ethel Davies; **60l** AA/Clive Sawyer; **60/61** AA/Clive Sawyer; **60r** AA/Clive Sawyer; **61l** AA/Clive Sawyer; **61r** AA/Clive Sawyer; **62l** AA/Julian Love; **62r** AA/Julian Love; **63l** AA/Julian Love; **63r** AA/Julian Love; **64t** AA/Clive Sawyer; **64b** Andre Jenny/Alamy; **65** AA/Clive Sawyer; **66** AA/Clive Sawyer; **67** Photodisc; **68** Pete Bennett; **69** AA/Julian Love; **72** AA/Clive Sawyer; **73l** AA/Clive Sawyer; **73r** AA/Clive Sawyer; **74l** AA/Clive Sawyer; **74r** AA/Clive Sawyer; **75t** AA/Clive Sawyer; **75bl** AA/Ethel Davies; **75br** Andre Jenny/Alamy; **76** AA/Clive Sawyer; **77** AA/Ethel Davies; **78** Digital Vision; **79** AA/Clive Sawyer; **80** AA/Clive Sawyer; **81** AA/Clive Sawyer; **84l** AA/Ethel Davies; **84r** AA/Ethel Davies; **85** The Phillips Collection; **86l** Rock Creek Park; **86r** Rock Creek Park; **87t** AA/Clive Sawyer; **87b** AA/Clive Sawyer; **88t** AA/Clive Sawyer; **88b** AA/Ethel Davies; **89** AA/Clive Sawyer; **90** AA/Clive Sawyer; **91** AA/Clive Sawyer; **92** Brand X Pictures; **93** AA/Pete Bennett; **94** Brand X Pictures; **95** AA/Julian Love; **98** AA/Clive Sawyer; **98/99t** AA/Clive Sawyer; **98/99c** AA/Ethel Davies; **99** AA/Ethel Davies; **100l** AA/Ethel Davies; **100r** AA/Clive Sawyer; **101l** AA/Ethel Davies; **101r** AA/Ethel Davies; **102t** AA/Clive Sawyer; **102bl** AA/Neil Ray; **102br** Chuck Pefley/Alamy; **103t** AA/Ethel Davies; **103bl** AA/Ethel Davies; **103br** AA/Ethel Davies; **104** AA/Simon McBride; **105** Digital Vision; **106** AA/Clive Sawyer; **107** AA/Julian Love; **108t** AA/Clive Sawyer; **108tr** Photodisc; **108ct** AA/Clive Sawyer; **108cb** Photodisc; **108b** Photodisc; **109** AA/Clive Sawyer; **110** AA/Clive Sawyer; **111** AA/Clive Sawyer; **112** AA/Clive Sawyer; **113** AA/Julian Love; **114** AA/Clive Sawyer; **115** AA/Clive Sawyer; **116** AA/Clive Sawyer; **117** AA/Clive Sawyer; **118t** AA/Clive Sawyer; **118b** AA/Ethel Davies; **119t** AA/Clive Sawyer; **119b** AA/Ethel Davies; **120t** AA/Clive Sawyer; **120l** MRI Bankers Guide to Foreign Currency; **121** AA/Clive Sawyer; **122t** AA/Clive Sawyer; **112b** AA/Larry Porges; **123** AA/Clive Sawyer; **124t** AA/Clive Sawyer; **124bl** Getty Images; **124bc** AA/Clive Sawyer; **124/125** AA/Ethel Davies **125t** AA/Clive Sawyer; **125bc** AA/Clive Sawyer; **125br** AA

Every effort has been made to trace the copyright holders, and we apologise in advance for any accidental errors. We would be happy to apply corrections in the following edition of this publication.